The Art of Seduction

**Table of Contents**

# Chapter 1

## Attract women for seduction

*Each fellow needs to have the capacity to pull in ladies. You're in a bar with your amigos, having a couple drinks after work, and all of a sudden you recognize an attractive lady giving you the eye from over the room. You forget about it and continue schmoozing with your companions, yet then you see a second, exceptionally proclaimed look. You give yourself a brisk gusto talk, head over, and start a discussion with the lady.*

*The discussion begins off well; she appears to be intrigued and bubbly. You take the regular first experience course, asking her where she works, where she's from, and what she accomplishes for no particular reason. Exactly when you're beginning to feel sure, she starts checking out the room and quits adding to the discussion. You rapidly guide the talk to another point, trusting that it will end the uncomfortable quiet that is by all accounts developing. Be that as it may, it doesn't work. She takes a brief taste from her beverage, pardons herself to go to the restroom, and stays away for the indefinite future.*

*On the off chance that this transpires all the time, then this article is for you. Perused on and discover how you can draw in ladies and keep the discussion interesting.*

## 1. Ladies would prefer not to be met

*Rather than soliciting her from inquiries such as "where are you from" and "what do you accomplish for the sake of entertainment," put forth an authoritative expression or a chilly read. For instance, say "you're not from around here, are you?" or "you should be a legal advisor." This is an astounding strategy to keep the discussion from transforming into an exhausting meeting. Attempt to practice this strategy whenever you're in a bar since it's a vital behavioral segment to draw in ladies.*

## 2. Ladies are pulled in to solid men

*Try not to discuss how tired you are or that you had seasonal influenza a week back. Rather, specify things that show great wellbeing. For instance, advise her something amusing that happened when you went for a run or while you were at the exercise center.*

### 3. Try not to gloat

*It's extraordinary that you have a decent car and an awesome occupation, yet don't advise her that specifically. In spite of the fact that ladies are pulled in to riches, they are not pulled in to men who boast about it. The purpose for this is ladies can sense that a propensity to gloat likely comes from low certainty. Rather than boasting, recount to her an intriguing story that permits her to decode autonomously that you're effective.*

### 4. When you converse with a lady, make a point to have a casual body stance

*Unwind your shoulders and put your weight on one leg. Incline serenely against a divider or the bar if conceivable. Most critical of all, hold your beverage to your side, not before you. Men tend to hold their beverages immovably before their stomachs. This makes a counterfeit hindrance in the middle of you and the lady and blocks your capacity to draw in her. On the off chance that you can join these proposals, you will seem to be an a great deal more certain and attractive individual.*

### 5. Attempt to be somewhat secretive

*In the event that she makes inquiries, don't give her extensive, point by point answers. Rather, furnish her with signs about who you are and given her a chance to make sense of the rest. This will interest her and brief her to take in more about you.*

### 6. Ladies affection to pretend

*Humor her making so as to long for dream her your own right hand and giving her a lively request. Alternately imagine that you are an adoring couple and afterward say a final farewell to her when she says something that you don't care for. Tease her and advise her that on the off chance that she compensates for it, you may take her back.*

*These six tips just touch the most superficial layer of drawing in ladies. On the off chance that you really need to better your capacities, Love Systems suggests that you download the full length free report titled "Main 10 botches men make with ladies." You can get it promptly and privately conveyed to your inbox. Simply enter your email in the case at the highest point of the page and let the amusements start!*

# Chapter 2

## What do women want in men?

*Indeed, what ladies need still remains the unanswered inquiry over the globe. Be that as it may, men needn't lose trust in all is not lost. There are still a decent number of things that most ladies like. Here are a couple from the not insignificant rundown which can maybe offer you some assistance with making her fall head over heels in adoration with you. Take your pick to charm and impress her!*

## Superman:

*Women adoration to be ensured. So appear in a bigger number of routes than one to demonstrate that you will be her friend in need ought to your lady land in trouble! Ladies are dependably in wonder of men who can venture up in times of contentions. Make sure you get each open door that circumstance tosses at you.*

## Look great:

*Deodorant Ads might be going over the edge indicating men being tricked by ladies' aroma. In any case, the other way is likewise genuine. Pick a deo that suits you. Particularly in the event that it's your first date, it's best not to take a stab at anything trial. Comprehend what notices best on you. Keep in mind, what noticed glorious on your companion may stink on your skin! For everything relies on upon your personal stench. When you shower fragrance on your body, what you smell is a blend of the deo splash and your personal stench. Pick savvy.*

## Shocks in abundance:

*Women love astonishments be it chocolates, love notes, blessings or even a bunch of blooms. Ladies don't worry about them in any numbers. You are certain to score brownie focuses with this one!*

### Straightforwardness:

*Honesty is still the best approach. Never mislead her in the event that you are thinking about a long haul relationship. Don't worry about it you will confront some starting fire, yet in the long run you will win over her trust.*

### Immaculate body:

*What with the big names being fixated on getting a six pack or eight pack abs, young ladies too go ga over men with a very much conditioned body. Get into the propensity for consistent workout so you can make heads turn!*

### Dress well:

*Nothing kills a ladies than a plain man. Do a style-check, detect the patterns in design, identify with a beautician to discover what looks best on you. Garments maketh man truly!*

### Delegated eminence:

*Nothing like an offbeat hair style! A decent haircut can give you an alternate look by and large. What are you sitting tight for? Understand that shocker look so you can inspire that chick you have been peering toward.*

*Enchantment of your hands:*

*You may have taken your better half to the most sizzling eateries around the local area, yet she wouldn't fret on the off chance that you can cook one of her most loved dishes (or even plain moment noodles) when she's eager. Such minutes are always remembered.*

*There's a joke doing the rounds that 'A lady's psyche is cleaner than a man's That's since she transforms it all the more frequently'. In any case, there are a few things that stay steady.*

*There are decent folks and there are awesome folks. Discover what ladies need in a man and what it takes to be an incredible gentleman that all ladies cherish and covet. A great deal of folks are really confounded about what ladies need in a man. Ladies are actually attracted to a few men, and similarly, ladies can't resist the urge to float away from some other men. So what makes a gentleman an incredible fellow and what makes him a bystander? Here are ten characteristics of an extraordinary gentleman that all ladies love. So on the off chance that you need to comprehend what ladies need in a man, utilize this agenda and be the man each lady would love to have as her own.*

*Presently a couple folks might whimper about the rundown being pretty darn hard on a fellow, yet normally it will be a really threatening rundown. You can't get to be one of the best folks on earth by going out for a stroll in the recreation center, right? Also, now we should jump carelessly into what ladies need in a man.*

## #1 A man who can regard her

*This might appear to be anything but difficult to do, yet do you truly regard your wife or sweetheart?*

*Most folks constantly view themselves as to be know-it-alls and accept they're superior to their lady inside and out. On the off chance that you think your lady's only an attractive eye candy, by what method would you be able to ever regard her? Regard must be earned, yes, however unless you really trust that your lady has some extraordinary qualities and is far better than you in a few viewpoints, you can never at any point regard her. Figure out how to regard the lady in your life, and she'll adore you and regard you significantly all the more as well.*

## #2 A man who can genuinely adore her

*You can blessing your wife or sweetheart with pricy doodads and extravagance get-aways, yet that is not so much the meaning of adoration [Read: The importance of love]. Genuine romance is partaken in little ways, each and every day. You don't have to enjoy open showcase of love or nestling each night while staring at the TV. Be that as it may, you have to tell your lady in little ways the amount she intends to you. [Read: How to better a relationship to thoroughly understand this]*

*When you're really enamored with your lady, satisfying her and trading off with both of your needs work out easily. Do you think about your lady's sentiments? Is it accurate to say that you are eager to catch wind of her day when you get back home? Do you anticipate investing energy with your lady after work or do you get more eager to play diversions or watch the TV? It's the seemingly insignificant details that truly matter, and every one of these signs appear.*

## #3 A man who can secure her

*Ladies, as autonomous as they might be, still love to be in the organization of a man they can depend upon in a tense circumstance. They need to feel ensured and dealt with, regardless of what the condition. Can you be that gentleman? Do you think your lady truly assumes that you can deal with any alarming circumstance you get into?*

## #4 A man that she can turn on to

*Do you revere or gaze toward anybody? All men have our own good examples, whether it's an opportunity warrior, a business investor, a NFL player or a weight lifter. You venerate them since those individuals have accomplished so much and move you to improve as a gentleman. On the off chance that you genuinely need to recognize what ladies need in a man, take care of business who can motivate individuals. You don't need to procure billions (would be extraordinary in the event that you could) or win the Nobel Prize, yet in the event that you could have any kind of effect in your own little ways, you could be that man. Be a decent speaker, an awesome conversationalist, an incredible pool player, or pretty much whatever else that is valuable in your life. For whatever length of time that your lady is awed with you for your aptitudes, she'll boast about it and adore you for it!*

## *#5 A man who is energetic*

*Ladies cherish a man who demonstrates a considerable measure of energy in bed, as well as in everything a man has confidence in. Energetic men are rousing and baffling, and ladies adore that.*

*You couldn't think less about an adventurer in the Amazonian wildernesses or Jack Sparrow on his capers, yet there's something so hot about these men. You don't comprehend what it is that makes them so energetic, and this puzzle just attracts ladies to them. Be energetic about something important, be it your entrepreneurial endeavor, your woodwork pastime or your tryst with composing a book or painting, and your lady will love you for the energy and enthusiasm you bring into her life.*

## #6 A man she can trust and rely on upon

*A reliable man who is tried and true is difficult to find, and that is the thing that makes these men so looked for after. It isn't so much that customary men can't be tried and true or dependable, it's simply that they couldn't care sufficiently less about anything to consider things important. What ladies need in a man is reliability. A reliable man doesn't let down his wife or sweetheart (however an uncommon event is passable), be it the basic need list or helping her alter her furniture. To be a tried and true man, you don't need every one of the answers. You simply should arrive for her, and help her in her season of need.*

## #7 A gallant man

*Gallantry is old fashioned, however's regardless it something all ladies cherish and venerate in a man. All men comprehend what it takes to be a gallant man, however shockingly, most men trust that being courageous is really an indication of being easygoing and making a decent attempt to satisfy a man. In any case, in opposition to what most men believe, being gallant is not an indication of shortcoming, rather it's an indication of admiration by both of the genders. By being courageous, it demonstrates that you regard the lady, and be responding to your valor, it demonstrates that the lady regards you.*

## *#8 A man who can prep himself*

*No doubt, we should hit the nuts and bolts once more. You need a shocking lady with bends such as a coke bottle, and a monstrosity in bed, and an incredible talker and a grimy talker, and so forth! What's more, genuinely, what are you offering her consequently, a Homer Simpson carbon copy? Truly?*

*So look, the world is reasonable the length of you play reasonable and concentrate on reality. What ladies need in a man is allure. On the off chance that you need to be with a lady who's all that you ever needed to be physically, you must do whatever you can to search bravo as well. Hit the exercise center frequently, go for a night run, or whatever works for you. Dress well and utilize a couple of masculine beautifying agents and rich colognes and fragrances. Resemble a big name in the city and ladies will trail you like you're a genuine big name!*

## *#9 A man who is yearning*

*Yearning folks could be giggled at, yet when they become wildly successful, they're the jeering ones who can say "who's chuckling now?!" Being yearning is simple, yet unless you make a move and work your direction towards your aspiration each and every day, who's going to care who you are. A goal-oriented fellow isn't a gentleman who considers awesome things, he's the fellow who does incredible things. Be this fellow and your lady and all other lady will love you and need you. Everybody loves a fellow who can prepare to stun the world and accomplish it. On the off chance that you can ever be this fellow, you're spot on top of the quality pool, and obviously, buddy, you're Mr. Compelling!*

## *#10 A man who can dream*

*What ladies what in a man is a visionary, be it a fantasizer in bed , a man who can imagine his effective future, or a man who can tell otherworldly stories while lazing on the loft and watching the stars with his darling. Ladies adore a man with a dynamic creative ability. Creative ability is such an extraordinary sidekick toward the end of an awful day, or while spending a sentimental minute together. It's sprightly, upbeat and such a burst of natural air. Inventive men make the best shocks, the most fascinating discussions and the happiest minutes in life. Truly, which lady won't love this fellow and which man can abstain from begrudging him?*

*Presently these ten qualities might appear to be really far away for some men. Be that as it may, as astonishing as it can appear to be, all these ten qualities that ladies adoration are inside of each and every man on earth. Yet, it's simply that they couldn't care sufficiently less to trust enough in themselves to be the best man they can be. A lady truly doesn't need much from a man. There are truly just seven things – seven qualities that she's searching for in an existence accomplice. Despite the fact that these qualities are elusive, they are characteristics of which each man is proficient. These seven things are not out of any man's span, yet the truth of the matter is that most need no less than one.*

*Presently, you might jump at the chance to contend that nobody is immaculate and in this manner nobody has every one of the seven of these qualities, yet that is simply not genuine. There are a lot of men out there who are adequate in each of these classes, not superbly, but rather sufficiently adequate to make a lady unbelievably glad. That is the only thing that is important, correct?*

### *1. Genuineness –*

*A lady doesn't need a man to mislead her about critical matters. She needs to be an imperative piece of his life – the most essential part, truth be told. She needs to know the things that are going on his life and she needs him to have trust in her. Similarly as she is concerned, they are one – his life is her life.*

*She needs him to need to partake in his charming encounters and recollections. She likewise doesn't need him to feel that he needs to lie, since when that is the situation it more often than not implies that he was venturing out of line, settling on poor decisions and botches. Then again, she doesn't need reality in all circumstances. Ruthless trustworthiness isn't needed.*

*On the off chance that she asks, she looks extraordinary, she looks lovely, the truth she picked up 15 pounds doesn't trouble you, her new hair style makes her look even cuter. Since I consider it, the main thing you should untruth is about such shallow matters as appearances. We all look like sh*t now and again – however she doesn't have to hear you say it.*

**2. Understanding** *– with the goal that she doesn't feel the need to account for herself.*

*She needs you to know her – all around. Why? Since at exactly that point will you adore her for her. We everything now and again need affirmation that we're worth adoring. The genuine us – not the general population others see us to be. We may not all need such an affirmation of our quality, yet we all need it. In any case, it's more than simply that.*

*Having somebody comprehend you is having somebody totally know you for the individual that you truly are. There's no disarray, there's no misconception or misguided judgment. They know you for you and in light of the fact that they know you for the individual you truly are, you, as it were, exist outside of yourself. For whatever length of time that they live on, so do you.*

**3. Importance**– *she needs to know she matters to you.*

*To be tended to implies not to be separated from everyone else in this life. A great many people are compelled to watch over themselves and actually it's significantly more troublesome than individuals let on. As individuals, we aren't generally in the right mentality to administer to ourselves. To finish it off, that is normally precisely when we require the most minding – when we aren't rationally or physically equipped for doing it without anyone's help.*

*She needs you to arrive for her when she needs somebody, to arrive to share her weight. I know it sounds silly, yet she needs you to make her life a little less demanding. Madness – I know. On the upside, she'll arrive for you when nobody else will. Sufficiently reasonable tradeoff I think.*

**4. Quality** – *both mental and physical.*

*No lady needs a physical weakling – it's against her inclination. That doesn't mean she won't make due with marginally not exactly Herculean, yet you're a man damn it. She needs to feel that when she's in your vicinity. She needs you to be clever and to practice poise basically in light of the fact that you can. We're all still creatures and ladies will dependably be pulled in to the more grounded men. She needs you to be solid not for the sole purpose of being solid – she needs you to be solid for her. It brings her pleasure, makes her vibe safe and turns her on. Do you genuinely require all the more persuading?*

**5. Sympathy** *– demonstrates her you're equipped for cherishing. A lady doesn't just need a man to have love just for her, yet an adoration forever, to live things. She needs a kind man, a man whom others will gaze upward to, acknowledge and respect. She needs a decent man.*

*She doesn't see being great and merciful as a shortcoming. What's more, that is on the grounds that it's most certainly not. I know bunches of men are taught that to be solid you must be contemptuous, angry and vindictive. That is exceptionally heartbreaking, yet it's just the world we live in. She needn't bother with that. You needn't bother with that either. Nobody does.*

**6. Security** *– monetary and exacting.*

*You don't should be a mogul. All things considered, for a few ladies, you extremely well might should be, yet ideally you'll just wind up with one who appreciates the attributes required for transforming oneself into a tycoon and not the cash alone. As a rule, the right lady will love you for you, however she needs you to make her vibe secure.*

*She needs to feel that you will shield her from physical damage. She needs to realize that you'll keep her protected, sound and agreeable. Does she require you to keep her safe? To bring home the bread? No. In any case, she'd like you to be fit for it – regardless of the possibility that her compensation is greater than yours. She'll have your back too so you can rest less demanding too.*

**7. Blind Loyalty** *– she needs to be the main lady he has eyes for. We all have enormous inner selves – men and ladies alike. We need to feel unique. We need to feel special and superior to the rest. We're aggressive by nature and there is no way to avoid it. Ladies need a man who sees the world in her. Her and just her. She knows she's not the most lovely or sharpest lady on the planet, however she doesn't should be – she's not fanciful. She simply needs you to think – know – that she's the most delightful, best lady on the planet for you.*

# Chapter 3

## The real art of seduction

*General public lives at a quickened pace and, keeping in mind the end goal to stay aggressive, men are regularly compelled to make moment suspicions and make prompt move with respect to vocation, buys, plans, and speculations. With regards to setting up a sexual relationship, things are the same. Not very many individuals have room schedule-wise important to completely evaluate another's character before jumping into a relationship. Rather, they depend on initial introductions and once in a while second-figure the thought that what they see from the begin is the thing that they'll generally get at last.*

*What's more, this is the reason it is so critical to make an awesome early introduction. The initial couple of snippets of contact turn into a measuring stick for each consequent impression you make. In only a few moments, a lady structures a first and enduring impression of you. Is it accurate to say that you are making a decent one? You would do well to trust so in light of the fact that there are no fresh opportunities with regards to making an extreme initial introduction. Everything that takes after relies on upon it.*

## *Start off on the right foot*

*Before I jump recklessly into the point, you should comprehend that there is no "flawless equation" that will suit or awe each lady. Be that as it may, while every individual has distinctive tastes and desires, there are a couple of basic qualities that pull in the female eye and ear more than others, and it's to your greatest advantage to ensure that you ingrain these characteristics in your conduct.*

*What you say, what you wear, your stance, your walk, your eye contact, your non-verbal communication, you're preparing propensities, your physical attributes, and a remarkable, beguiling, funny, and innovative methodology will begin you off on the right foot, however all that still isn't sufficient.*

## *what turns ladies off?*

*So also, there are some broad no-nos of dating convention and self-expression that ought to be kept away from. Ladies can be exceptionally unforgiving in case you're blameworthy of one of the accompanying:*

## *Appearance*

## Grimy hands

*According to ladies, unclipped, messy fingernails and unkempt hands, essentially, look disturbing. You comprehend what you need to do.*

## Bristly look

*Most ladies incline toward a clean-shaven man — that incorporates pubic hair. Get a hair style, keep it short. On the off chance that you have a facial hair, mustache or goatee, ensure it's trim. On the other hand, remember that, unless you're Magnum P.I., most ladies will believe that you have something to hole up behind all that facial hair.*

*The Caterpillar*

*Otherwise called the unibrow or It . Investigate the mirror. Do you have one eyebrow? Trust me when I let you know that ladies despise unibrows. Endless men go home alone in light of the caterpillars on their brows. Luckily, you can make a move . Have It professionally tweezed or waxed, or uproot it by means of electrolysis.*

## Out-dated glasses

*On the off chance that your goggles are over 7 years of age, it's an ideal opportunity to get another pair. You'd be shocked at what another pair of creator glasses can accomplish for your mug.*

## Dressing like a nerd

*You ought to constantly dress as indicated by your surroundings. In today's day and age, everything is with respect to your environment. Clearly, an understudy isn't relied upon to appear to class in a tuxedo. Nor if you acknowledge that your closest companion appears to a supper party in a sweat shirt and grimy pants. The thought is to continually add some in vogue strings to your closet, and keep your apparel clean and in great condition. You ought to likewise have a couple sets of in vogue shoes. Ladies can inform a great deal concerning a man by what he wears on his feet and how he administers to his shoes. Absolutely never wear shoes that are scratched, foul or in desperate need of a shine.*

## Yellow teeth

*Canary yellow teeth is one of the greatest side roads for everybody. It demonstrates that you're an apathetic person who can't keep his mouth clean. On the off chance that your teeth are yellow, overdo it on brightening gel and mouthpieces from your dental practitioner. Nothing is sexier than silvery whites.*

## Personal stench

*The way you smell is an essential variable that pulls in the women, so unless she's dependent on the scent of onions and sewer, ensure you don't possess an aroma similar to it. Noticing great begins with scrubbing down and keeping away from sustenances that cause undesirable smells. A planner cologne wouldn't hurt either. Simply ensure you're not attempting to cover a dreadful smell with it.*

## State of mind

### No desire

*It's hard to believe, but it's true, you're uneducated, unemployed, you invest your free energy (which happens to be 24 hours a day) playing computer games, you owe cash to each one of your companions, and the most exceedingly terrible piece of everything is that you're content with your life and anticipate that ladies will acknowledge you for who you are. All things considered, continue envisioning since ladies are normally pulled in to men with aspirations and objectives. What's more, in case you're fulfilled by your extraordinary employment, reconsider in light of the fact that that will get exhausting as well. Ladies love men who are always shooting for the stars.*

### Poor conduct

*Chatting with your mouth full, cleaning out your nose at the table, not utilizing a blade and fork when proper, and neglecting to haul the seat out for a woman during supper are certain flame approaches to get rejected.*

## *Reviling*

*Utilizing slang or revile words shows an absence of insight. There are a ton of words in the English dialect that can express what is on your mind without your resorting to reviling. When you talk utilizing indecency, ladies will reject you and you'll never be considered important. Too, swearing shows that your vocabulary is restricted.*

## *Examining past encounters*

*Discussing exes or more awful, exes, whether positive or negative, is a kiss of death. Nobody needs to contend nor would they like to be around a wolf in sheep's clothing.*

## *Unnecessarily shoddy*

*Going Dutch on a first date, not tipping, never purchasing a round of beverages, and rationalizing not to go out on the town keeping in mind the end goal to spare cash, will persuade her to be somewhat more efficient with the time she designates to you.*

## As yet living at home

*Unless you're Italian, a lady will never comprehend why a man who's more than 30 still lives at home with mother and daddy. Get your own particular flat and figure out how to be capable.*

## A whiner

*Nobody can remain to associate with somebody who gripes about everything: awful nourishment, awful administration, messy hair day, terrible climate, awful family, awful exes, awful companions, awful employment... Aieee , I'm beginning to get discouraged.*

## A terrible conversationalist

*Talking gradually makes you sound doltish. Talking rapidly will make you sound anxious and frail. Take as much time as is needed and annunciate your words appropriately keeping in mind the end goal to appear to be an astute individual.*

*Constrained extension*

*You ought to think around somewhat more than simply wrestling, football, hockey, b-ball, and bosoms. In the event that you need ladies to be occupied with what you need to say, you have to advise yourself about current undertakings and build up your own particular scholarly feeling.*

## Egotistical

*Give her a chance to discover what an extraordinary fellow you are all alone and in due time. The exact opposite thing she needs to hear is the amount of cash you make, what an extraordinary auto you drive, what sort of occupation you have, and how huge your penis is in the initial five minutes of discussion. Keep in mind, nobody prefers a big talker.*

*Beyond any doubt it's enjoyable to be a tease and discuss sexual dreams with a lady you want, yet not on a first experience — particularly in the event that she doesn't bring it up. On the off chance that she suspects your diversion and supposes you're a player, the amusement is over.*

## Alcoholic

*The exact opposite thing a lady needs is to be hassled and attacked by a tanked man who supposes he's telling so as to help her out her that she has an incredible as, when all he truly needs to advise her is that he'd like her telephone number. When you begin to slur and go cross-looked at, individuals will believe you're a drunkard who can't control himself.*

*With such a variety of men to rival, it's just typical that you need to make an extraordinary early introduction keeping in mind the end goal to stand out enough to be noticed. In any case, I'm certain that is something you as of now perceive. Truth be told, I'll wager that you're pondering internally, Tell me something I don't definitely know. Indeed, in case you're going to learn something today, it ought to be this: An initial introduction happens each time you help out the first run through, and it's that impression she will never forget.*

*For instance, she may surmise that you're an amusing gentleman since you made her chuckle the first occasion when you talked. Be that as it may, she'll likewise believe you're a weakling in the event that you begin to cry since you tumbled off your bicycle the first occasion when you took her bicycle riding. What's more, regardless of what you do starting there on, she'll consider you powerless.*

*That is the reason you need to leave an enduring impression each time you experiment.*

*Most men believe that an initial introduction happens just on the first experience. All things considered, I have news for you; on the grounds that a lady falls for the delegate you at first present, that doesn't mean she'll quit examining you. Ladies are exceptionally mindful of the "agent" element and that initial introductions can be deceiving, that is the reason they're continually trying men.*

*Keep in mind; there's an initial introduction for everything. You leave an early introduction when you first approach, on the first date, the first move, when you meet her loved ones, the first kiss, when you first uproot your dress, your first sexual experience together, and your first battle. What's more, that is the reason you generally must know about your activities and how they may influence other individuals and their judgments of you.*

## Chapter 4

### The importance of eye contact

*It is a subject for which there is a stunning measure of confounding guidance. What's more, in light of current circumstances. Somebody can show you how to physically stroll up to a lady, what to verbally say in a discussion and even, to a specific degree, how to touch her.*

*Be that as it may, it is extremely hard to instruct folks how to do things with their eyes. I'm great companions with one of the best folks on the planet with regards to ladies, Cory Skyy. He does a large portion of his pickup with eye contact alone. Be that as it may, next to no of what he educates is the genuine mechanics of eye contact. It's excessively confounded and depends so vigorously on internal amusement, which he teaches.*

*Eye contact is firmly identified with methodology nervousness in that for timid folks, it boils down to one thing: strife evasion. One of the signs of social nervousness is eye stare shirking.*

*Various studies bolster this. Individuals with social nervousness have a tendency to experience issues holding eye contact. My companion Kelvin, who has managed social nervousness for quite a long time, discusses his repugnance for eye contact. "I have dependably experienced issues looking at individuals without flinching. I don't was damaged in a specific manner including eye contact, however I generally had a, hard time looking at individuals without flinching."*

*"I relate looking at individuals without flinching with individuals being super distraught at me. I feel scared, similar to they are either passing judgment on me super hard, or they are about prepared to punch me. That is only sort of my gut response at whatever time I look at somebody without flinching, unless they are simply super smiley or super cheery." Eye contact is characteristically fixing to certainty. It is in our science. At the point when clashes happen, creatures "show" themselves keeping in mind the end goal to show strength.*

*At the point when showing in a contention, a creature will evaluate his rival and himself. On the off chance that he sees his rival to be more prevailing, he gives way. This permits rank request to shape. Rank progression is a vital abhorrence among creatures to diminish strife and take into consideration creatures with contending hobbies to exist together in relative concordance. At the point when a creature "gives way," he flags to the next that he is compliant. These accommodating signs are stereotyped for any given species and are shockingly predictable on up through the developmental chain. In The Evolution of Depression, Paul Gilbert notes The beginnings of our story do a reversal far. Both reptiles and feathered creatures structure positions which bring about responsibility for rearing domain. At the point when challenges for domain happen, there is a specific sort of interactional showcase. To begin with, the candidates confront one another and stand erect, firm legged, and/or puff themselves up; they take part in what is called ceremonial agonistic conduct. This might be a stand-off circumstance and still happens in people, for example, standing erect and meeting eye stare, particularly when there is to be a physical challenge (e.g., in boxing, wrestling, and American football maybe). To keep up eye stare in such circumstances is to demonstrate an absence of apprehension. This is an extremely primitive force signal. It permits the person to work out if the challenger confronting them is more grounded or weaker and after that react suitably. It's entirely imperative that the creature understands that judgment of similar quality right, not just to abstain from getting into or dragging out hazardous battles, additionally to challenge those circumstances that it could win and be socially fruitful in.*

*So how improve eye contact?*

*As you enhance your internal amusement and fabricate certainty through drawing closer ladies, your eye contact will actually progress.*

*Until then, here are ten tips to concentrate on.*

## *When you look at a lady*

*you don't have the foggiest idea, let her turn away first. Work on holding eye contact with individuals longer. Begin with your companions. At that point begin giving more eye contact to outsiders. On the off chance that you meet eyes with a lady, attempt to give her a chance to look path before you do.*

## *2. When you look away,*

*don't think back for a small amount of a second. Individuals with low-certainty tend to take a gander at a man, turn away, and afterward think back again quickly. This is a "checking" movement. It indicates destitution since you are verifying what the other individual is doing as opposed to being sure about yourself.*

## 3. Unwind and have a wonderful look

*all over. When you do look at somebody help up your face. Put on a clue of a grin or if nothing else unwind your face however much as could be expected. You need it to look warm, welcoming and lovely, maybe how it would look on the off chance that you were conversing with a companion. On the off chance that ladies are getting creeped out or continually turning away, it's imaginable you are excessively exceptional. To ease up on the power when you look, take a stab at looking tenderly past her, as though you are taking a gander at the space behind her as opposed to gazing her in the eyes.*

**4. Give much eye contact** *as could be expected when in discussion. When you are in a discussion and the other individual is talking, look at them without flinching 100% of the time. It's alright to turn away more in case you're talking–but don't float off for a really long time. When you are talking, look at the other individual in the eye 70-100% of the time. It's additionally alright to turn away when you are clowning around with her or teasing her.*

## 5. When in a gathering

*dependably take a gander at whom ever is talking. You don't generally need to be the focal point of consideration. It's alright to give other individuals the spotlight. Yet, you need to ensure that you take a gander at whom ever is talking at the time. In the event that you are looking somewhere else, you seem to be hermitic and separated.*

## 6. Getting eye contact

*is about what you do with your entire body. The amount of eye get in touch with you get from ladies will have more to do with your non-verbal communication than the way you move your eyes. In the event that you are strolling with a certain swagger, you will get more eye contact. Ladies notice you from a mile away, likely before you even notice them. What's more, what they see is the manner by which you move. They perceive how you conduct yourself.*

*I get a kick out of the chance to picture that I possess the spot, that I'm strolling around ensuring everybody is having a great time. I additionally some of the time imagine that I'm a cop, that I possess the street and I'm looking past every one of these regular people for something vital. Essentially the thought is that you are a big cheese.*

## 7. Get Comfortable Being Seen

. Eye contact is needy more on how you respond to individuals when they take a gander at you, as opposed to what you look like at other individuals. Sure folks are ordinarily the pioneers of their gathering. Everybody in the gathering is looking to them to witness what's going to next. The sure folks ingests the look of everyone around him. He appreciates it. You can work on taking so as to get happy with being seen up a considerable measure of space.

While strolling I get a kick out of the chance to picture is that I'm not letting individuals move beyond me on the walkway. How might you walk on the off chance that you didn't need individuals to pass you? You would make yourself greater. When I stroll into a room, I stroll through the focal point of it, regardless of the possibility that it's vacant. In case I'm sitting with a gathering of individuals, I choose the center of the gathering.

## 8. Keep your eyes at the skyline level

*or above rather than looking down. Looking down is connected with disgrace and yielding to a predominant. Picture youngsters when they get in a bad position and a grown-up is hollering at them. They hang their head in disgrace and look down. You need to do the opposite. Attempt to keep your look at the skyline level or above. Especially when you look away from individuals, don't look down, look to the either side.*

## *9. While drawing nearer a lady*

*, don't gaze at her. At the point when strolling over to a lady to converse with her, make an effort not to concentrate a lot on her. This is just on the grounds that it's threatening. She can feel you gazing at her and it puts her protections up. When I approach, I go about as though I were glancing around for something and am going to approach her for bearings. Regardless of the possibility that she's not taking a gander at you, she can even now feel somebody's eye stare on her and it might crack her out. You certainly need to give her eye contact when you get to her. In any case, take a stab at turning away for a bit before you get to her.*

## *10. Try not to sit tight for eye contact*

*to approach. In the event that I sat tight for eye contact before I drew nearer, I would never approach anybody. I was never great at the eye contact amusement and I drew closer and dated numerous ladies. I started to get significantly more eye contact after I began drawing nearer. The drawing nearer made me sure and ladies could sense that. They were pulled in to that. Learn as much as you can about eye contact however don't depend on it. On the off chance that you are as yet taking in the signs you will in any case need to way to deal with see whether you are perusing the signs effectively.*

*There are truly no firm principles with regards to eye contact. Attempt some distinctive things and see what works for you. Each individual is distinctive.*

*You likewise don't have to utilize your tongue. That is for more experienced kissers.*

*Lesson #8: Savor the Moment and Slowly Let Go*

*When you bolt your lips, appreciate the experience. You've done it! You are in your first kiss - AH! How magnificent is that?*

*At the point when does it end? No compelling reason to tally. Simply hold up a little and after that gradually move your head back a bit. Your kissing accomplice will comprehend that the kissing is over and move his or her head back as well.*

*As you move back, gradually open your head, investigate the eyes of your kissing accomplice and grin.*

*Sneak in a speedy little kiss once you isolate from the lips. It's charming and demonstrates that you truly enjoyed the kiss. It will send an additional little shudder down his or her spine.*

*You're Ready for Your Kiss*

*You have the information now to kiss somebody and with this learning, you have the force. Take it and use it to make a standout amongst the most huge snippets of your life. Your apprehensions will soon be behind you when you have your first ever kiss. You'll need to do it now and again, so it should be present here. It's really regular for timid or socially cumbersome sorts to say they experience difficulty holding eye contact with individuals. Some run of the mill explanations behind this are:*

*On the off chance that somebody is timid they might discover it feels excessively exceptional and scaring, making it impossible to look at a man without flinching.*

*Additionally, on the off chance that somebody is socially on edge, by not taking a gander at somebody's face they can "uproot" one stream of social incitement and make the connection feel less overpowering.*

*In case you're not accustomed to it, it requires push to intentionally attempt to look at individuals without flinching while likewise addressing or listening to them. It's somewhat like attempting to pat your head and rub your stomach in the meantime. By not looking you can evacuate that wellspring of diversion and put more concentrate on forming your musings or contemplating what the other individual is stating.*

*For a few individuals looking is essentially as a negative behavior pattern they've fallen into. Perhaps their guardians and instructors never taught them to look at others without flinching when they were more youthful.*

*A few individuals tend to daydream and lose all sense of direction in their heads when they're mingling. Not looking is an impact of that.*

*Essentially everybody will let you know eye contact is an imperative part of correspondence. It makes you seem to be more drawn in, agreeable, and certain. Likewise, it furnishes you with a considerable measure of non-verbal data about what the other individual is thinking and feeling. By turning away you miss all that. Another advantage is that looking compels you to put some of your mental vitality into concentrating on other individuals, which implies you have less left over to get latched onto your subconscious mind and think unreliable musings. The following are a few tips on the most proficient method to figure out how to get more happy with looking at others:*

*You may be looking than you might suspect*

*It's absolutely conceivable that in case you're scanning for help on the most proficient method to look that you truly do turn away excessively. On the off chance that individuals have reached is poor, then this is certainly the case. Be that as it may, I'll put this point out there in light of the fact that occasionally individuals feel like they're not looking, but rather they really are. When they identify with individuals they're by and large looking toward them and appear to be mindful, but since they don't feel like they're always mindful of looking at other individuals specifically without flinching, they accept they're not doing what's necessary.*

*You can fulfill a considerable amount without looking*

*Things being what they are, looking is superior to not doing it, but rather I'd scarcely say it's a component that will totally represent the moment of truth your social achievement. On the off chance that somebody has a number of different things going for them socially, the way that they now and then turn away from somebody while they're conversing with them won't be an immense arrangement. In the event that you wish your eye contact was better then by all methods take a shot at it, yet don't obsess about it excessively.*

*Attempt to get into the propensity for looking steadily, not at the same time*

*It can be precarious to look at individuals when you're not accustomed to it. As I specified, it can feel scaring and rationally depleting. What here and there happens is somebody will set out to look away propensity. They'll begin looking at individuals without flinching reliably, and have the capacity to keep it up for a week or two, through resolution and the oddity of dealing with something new. At that point they'll slip back to their old ways.*

*It might be more useful to gradually work your way up to making a strong measure of eye contact. It will require investment before looking turns into a programmed, easy aptitude. Try not to anticipate that yourself will go from 0 to 100% overnight and afterward never about-face. It's the same as how somebody who eats inadequately typically can't simply drop everything one day and switch to a ultra-sound eating routine. The focuses underneath will go into more insight about some sub-abilities you can chip away at.*

*Have a go at utilizing the TV as practice*

*You don't need to begin with genuine individuals. When you're sitting in front of the TV attempt to look at all the characters on the screen the way you'd concentrate on a conversational accomplice, all things considered. News indicates where the moderator looks and talks right to you have a tendency to be the best. Talk appears with various visitors can likewise be helpful in light of the fact that it can get you used to changing your consideration from speaker to speaker. This can all give you a decent estimate of what it's similar to do it, all things considered. You can likewise think about the different ways individuals utilize their eyes to convey.*

*Give your eye contact muscles time to get into shape*

*When you look at somebody you need to continue taking a gander at a particular zone. Not just does your lens need to concentrate on something a specific separation away, yet you additionally need to utilize your eye attachment muscles to hold your eyes up. Your neck and general stance likewise must be in a position where you can look at the other individual in the eye. When you're not looking you're frequently not doing any of these things. You're normally looking more down, or up and to the side, and your eyes might be unfocused as you're lost in your considerations.*

*When you attempt to look at individuals the majority of the sudden, your muscles most likely won't be up to the undertaking. You'll discover your eyes get tired from having to really concentrate on someone else. This is one reason it can take a while to add to the propensity. Once more, rehearsing on the TV can help with this. Attempt to take a shot at the less demanding parts of eye contact first I think we all naturally comprehend that a few sorts of eye contact are less demanding than others: Looking at somebody right without flinching is perfect, however in the event that you look some place close-by, the other individual won't have the capacity to tell. You might discover it a considerable measure less demanding to look between the individual's eyes, or marginally above them to begin with.*

*It's much less demanding to look when you're listening to somebody versus when you're the speaker. When you're listening you simply need to kick back and concentrate on the other individual. When you're talking, a great deal of your mental vitality goes into considering what to say in the occasion. That is the reason individuals for the most part don't look when they're talking. You could begin by just attempting to look when you're the audience, and after that work on the talking part later.*

*It's less demanding to look for a brief timeframe versus an amid longer discussion. When you're learning you could begin off by just attempting to look for fast, 'discard' discussions with individuals such as clerks. It's simpler to look at individuals who don't scare you. Like a great many people, you likely get more bothered looking an appealing or high-status individual in the eye contrasted with visiting to your folks or companions. You could let yourself know that it's alright in the event that you can't look at additionally forcing individuals immediately, and that you'll take a shot at that later.*

*Presently you might discover it feels like a lot work to deliberately arrange for when you'll look at individuals and when you won't. By and by you might simply attempt to look as could be expected under the circumstances, not get down on yourself over the times you can't, and gradually get more accustomed to it. Be that as it may, on the off chance that you discover you experience difficulty procuring the propensity, taking a more deliberate methodology is dependably an alternative.*

*Give an excessive amount of eye contact, and you seem to be excessively extraordinary, (best case scenario) or a dreadful starer (even from a pessimistic standpoint). Give too little eye contact, and the other individual may contemplate what they need to say. Additionally, when you're stressing over looking, whatever remains of the connection endures. Rather than getting a charge out of an incredible discussion, you're focusing about eye contact.*

## The Secret Of Great Eye Contact

*Luckily, there's a straightforward trap that will offer you ace incredible eye some assistance with contacting. Simply coordinate your eye contact with your partner's. On the off chance that they take a gander at you, take a gander at them. In the event that they turn away, turn away. Simple, isn't that so?*

*Here's the reason it works. There's no such thing as "impeccable" eye contact. You will likely make your accomplice feel great with you, which implies you should do nothing more than abstain from giving an excess of eye contact or insufficient. Diverse individuals feel great with various levels of eye contact. In any case, practically everyone will start the measure of eye contact that they feel great with. That implies that on the off chance that you give them the same measure of eye contact that they give you, they'll most likely feel great. Take a gander at your accomplice when they take a gander at you (and turn away when they don't), and you'll be soundly inside the level of eye contact they feel great with. It truly is that simple. Mastering Good Eye Contact Obviously, there are a couple points of interest to deal with.*

*You would prefer not to reflect your accomplice precisely, or they'll rapidly acknowledge you're duplicating them. It's alright to in a flash match their eye contact once in a while, however by and large, you ought to hold up a few moments before duplicating them. Hold up around one second before taking a gander at them, and around a few seconds before turning away. Those numbers are simply unpleasant rules, obviously. Don't hesitate to investigation to discover what feels regular for you. The critical thing is that you abstain from moving such as a mirror picture of your accomplice. The precise timing of your delays is less vLikewise, know that eye contact rules change to some degree when you're having an enthusiastic discussion. It's occasionally simpler to examine intense subject matters when you're not taking a gander at somebody, so when individuals are sharing something extremely individual or enthusiastic, they will in some cases turn away from the individual they are identifying with.*

*On the off chance that that happens, regardless you have to take a gander at them to demonstrate that you give it a second thought. In the event that your look meanders, that imparts that you don't generally think about what they're stating, which is terrible whenever yet particularly frightful when they're sharing something enthusiastic.*

## *Eye Contact Rhythm*

*As you begin coordinating your accomplice's eye contact, you'll begin to add to a feeling of the amount of eye contact feels "regular." Eventually, you won't have to intentionally consider coordinating their eye contact - it will simply happen naturally. On the off chance that you need to speed that procedure, there's a simple approach to show signs of improvement feeling of the "mood" of eye contact. Simply observe a few films and pay consideration on the eye contact given between the characters. That will offer you some assistance with seeing what sort of eye contact coordinating looks characteristic. Remember that distinctive settings lead to various types of eye contact. Two being a tease significant others may coordinate eye contact moves immediately and have more drawn out eye contact, though two associates may take a few seconds to match one another and turn away regularly. Additionally, when you investigate the film connections you may see that characters won't coordinate one another 100% - some of the time one character will take a gander at another despite the fact that the other character is as yet turning away. This is absolutely alright.*

*Everything you need is a comparable level of eye contact. There's no compelling reason to coordinate their eye contact impeccably. In the event that now and again you have a craving for taking a gander at them despite the fact that they're not taking a gander at you, or you have a craving for turning away before they do, that is fine. The imperative thing is that you are "when all is said in done" coordinating what they do. For whatever length of time that you're in the same ballpark as them, then your eye contact will be fine. When you're beginning, you'll need to coordinate their eye contact intently to ensure that you stay in the protected zone. Yet, as you acquire experience, you'll show signs of improvement feeling of what eye contact level feels regular. That will give you a chance to modify your eye contact to what feels good for both you and them, not simply them.*

*The deciding result is that you won't need to consider eye contact by any stretch of the imagination - you'll simply do the eye contact that feels regular for both you and your accomplice. Take a touch of time to take in these great eye contact methods, and you'll get yourself lavishly remunerated with more agreeable and charming discussions for both you and your accomplices.*

*At the point when your accomplice takes a gander at you, take a gander at them. When they turn away, turn away Stop for a few moments before coordinating your accomplice's eye contact .As you grow more experience, you won't have to coordinate your accomplice's eye contact as precisely in light of the fact that you can depend on your impulses.*

## Chapter 5

### How to make everlasting first impression

### 1. Try not to Make Too Many Gestures.

*In the event that the message that you are attempting to send is one of certainty, control, and concentrate then don't keep running up to a lady waving your hands and jerking your body like you have an excessive amount of vitality. This sort of development sends the message that you are not happy in your own body. It additionally makes ladies uncomfortable to be close you.*

*What you need to do is keep your body in control and have a casual air about you. You ought to utilize motions, however utilize them when proper. This will communicate something specific that you are in control and will be a quiet, sure individual to be around.*

*Take in more about utilizing your non-verbal communication to draw in ladies here*

## *2. Keep up a Confident Posture.*

*Early introduction: Being Confident Makes A Huge Difference*

*Try not to approach a lady drooped over, arms crossed, and eyes confronting towards the floor. It doesn't make a difference how great of a discussion you keep up with her, this sort of body acting will talk about low self-assurance or a negative mentality. In any case, it's not an alluring position.*

*Hold yourself high, pull your shoulders back, keep your head up, and communicate something specific that you are a man who is deserving of other individuals' consideration and fondness. That is the sort of early introduction pose that will leave a lady needing to meet you once more.*

## 3. Be Positive, But Not Too Positive.

*A negative fellow who grumbles about everything under the sun is not going to make a decent initial introduction. That sort of gentleman will have ladies tallying during the time until they can make tracks in an opposite direction from them, and after that make them never think back. Try not to be negative amid your initial introduction, as ladies will be expecting your best conduct, and a negative state of mind ought not be your best conduct.*

*Having an inspirational state of mind is continually going to win over a lady's feeling about you. Simply ensure you don't try too hard. On the off chance that you are singing about daylight and candies, then you can have all the earmarks of being somewhat insane. Simply send the message that you cherish life and that you are a glad individual.*

## 4. Keep up Eye Contact.

*When you are identifying with a lady surprisingly, look at her without flinching. On the off chance that you are tricky with your eyes, or taking a gander at anything or anybody however her eyes, then you are passing on one of two messages. The principal message is that you couldn't care less about their vicinity and that you are amazingly exhausted with them. The second message is that you are effectively occupied. Both of the messages is going to leave a terrible initial introduction with a lady. To make a decent initial introduction with them, ensure you keep up a proper measure of eye contact.*

## 5. Discuss Relevant Things.

*Amid an early introduction, you would prefer not to discuss things you ordinarily talk about with your companions. Anything that is close to home ought to be stayed away from. The lady you are conversing with does not know your convictions and values and, in this way, can't gage what you are truly attempting to say when you talk in regards to how disturbed you feel today.*

*Discuss your environment. Discuss the things you have in like manner. Discuss the individual sitting alongside you. Simply keep the discussion important and evade data that is excessively individual.*

## 6. Watch out for Her Body Language.

*In the event that you need to gage what sort of impression you are making on her, watch her non-verbal communication. On the off chance that she is moving in an opposite direction from you, collapsing her arms, or raising her eyebrows, then you might be making an awful initial introduction and need to modify your tone, discussion, or non-verbal communication. Then again, on the off chance that she is grinning, loose, and looking at you, then you are presumably making a decent initial introduction and you can simply continue doing what you are doing.*

## 7. Make inquiries.

*When you are not making inquiries, you are in all likelihood discussing yourself, your feelings, or your convictions. When you speak a lot about yourself, you can have all the earmarks of being narrow minded. An egotistical state of mind is a major turn off amid an initial introduction.*

*Take a stab at making inquiries to seem intrigued by her. The more you permit her to discuss herself, or impart her insights and convictions, the more she will see you as somebody who really thinks about her and what she needs to say. You will dependably leave ladies (and other individuals) needing to see you again on the off chance that you can demonstrat to them that you think about them.*

## 8. Be Authentic.

*Amid an initial introduction, you might should be somewhat more formal in your discussion, however regardless you must be true. Try not to concur with something you can't help contradicting just to inspire a lady. Try not to talk in a way that you think will awe her when it conflicts with the way you ordinarily talk. You will improve an impression in the event that you remain by your ethics and convictions and stay consistent with the individual you are. (Simply ensure you don't push your thoughts on another person or they might mark you as domineering.)*

## 9. Be Well-Mannered

*No one likes a rude individual. In the event that you are impolite, self-important, or rude then you will leave an awful taste in her mouth, and she will name you as somebody that she wouldn't like to meet once more. Ensure you are respectful and contemplate her sentiments and the sentiments of other individuals around you. Being neighborly will demonstrat to them that you are aware of other individuals and that you have passionate insight.*

## 10. Be Well Groomed.

*This might appear glaringly evident, yet there are ordinarily that we can exit the entryway without a worry about our presentation and make numerous awful early introductions along the way. Individuals judge brutally in light of appearance, and regardless of the possibility that you are very much mannered, scholarly, and entertaining amid an initial introduction, individuals will even now base a larger part of their feeling in transit you dress and look.*

*It doesn't make a difference on the off chance that you don't think you are going to keep running into a lady or not, generally go out dressed to inspire with a specific end goal to make the best initial introduction wherever you go.*

## 11. Keep The Conversation Going.

*On the off chance that you don't have anything to say, and there are numerous clumsy quiets in your discussion, then you will most likely make an ungainly initial introduction that will leave a lady not having any desire to need to experience another uncomfortable meeting with you. You don't need that to happen! So you need to keep the discussion streaming.*

*Discovering things to discuss is not that hard. You should simply listen to the lady who is conversing with you, and make note of any strange references they say amid the discussion. Anything that they specify will be something that they appreciate, consider, or know about. It can be a reference around a man, spot, or occasion.*

*For instance, on the off chance that it is down-pouring outside, and she says how the downpour will be useful for patio nurseries, then she likely has some kind of fascination towards gardens. When you are stuck for discussion, raise that reference that she made about greenery enclosures, and she will presumably have a ton to say in regards to them.*

*Utilize the above 11 tips to offer you some assistance with making the most out of your initial introduction. Never take the initial introduction gently. On the off chance that you make a decent impression, you can leave ladies needing to see you once more. Furthermore, on the off chance that you don't make a decent impression, you can demolish your odds of making another impression by any means.*

# Chapter 6

## Always make your first kiss a memorable one

*It's the ideal opportunity for your first kiss. Try not to sweat it. It's not as hard as you think. When you do it a couple times, you'll recollect and ponder, "What on the planet was I so apprehensive going to start with..." The trap is to get by the first-run through nerves.*

## Your First Kiss Fears

*In case you're having some uneasiness about your first kiss, you aren't the only one. Everybody has some trepidation when it comes time to pucker up surprisingly. What do a great many people stress over?*

## Will she think I am a decent kisser?

*Imagine a scenario in which it's startling and my breath notices awful. I have never kissed anybody. I don't comprehend what to do. In what capacity will I know he or she needs to kiss me? Imagine a scenario in which we knock heads. Which way do I turn my head? What amount of tongue do I utilize? Do I utilize my tongue? Where do I put my hands? To what extent do I kiss for? In what manner will I know when to stop? At the point when do I turn my head amid a kiss? Do I turn my head? It's alright. You won't need to know everything about kissing when you kiss interestingly on the grounds that learn to expect the unexpected. Your first kiss won't be a 20 minute make-out session.*

*You will in all probability have a five second (if that) kissing session that will comprise of two lips puckered that touch one another with some suction. That is it. You'll discharge, investigate one another's eyes and you'll believe it's enchanted. Your kissing accomplice will most likely believe it's really great as well.*

*While this might appear to be really basic, that doesn't mean you shouldn't be furnished with a few tips before you enter your first kissing knowledge.*

## The Lowdown on Your First Kiss

*It's the ideal opportunity for some kissing training. While this sets you up to kiss interestingly, the most ideal approach to idealize your kissing method is to do it. Careful discipline brings about promising results - so once you know how to kiss, don't be reluctant to pucker up when the minute calls for it.*

## Lesson #1: Invest in Mints

*Have mints on hands at all times. You can without much of a stretch swallow a mint when you're going to kiss somebody. That way, you can be guaranteed that your breath is new and clean.*

## Lesson #2: How to Know When to Kiss

*You'll know somebody needs to kiss you when the individual looks profoundly at you and inclines toward you. You'll feel it inside you that there's something going to happen. On the off chance that you begin inclining toward the individual, and he or she doesn't venture back or recline, you know it's time...a exceptional time for a kiss.*

## Lesson #3: Imagine Kissing

*At this moment, attempt it. Envision kissing the individual you think you'll be kissing surprisingly. Pay consideration on where your hands will go.*

*More often than not, they go on the individual's waist, or in case you're grasping, amidst your accomplice's back. On the off chance that you are sitting beside one another, it's alright to hold his or her hand(s), or place a hand on the arm, or upper thigh.*

## Lesson #4: Relax Your Body

*Take a full breath and let it hard and fast, so your body is casual. On the off chance that you are excessively concerned, your lips will stay tight, and you're kissing accomplice will feel that. Recall that, you can do this.*

## Lesson #5: Move Slowly Into the Kiss

*To determine your nervousness about which approach to move your head, move in gradually for the kiss. That way, you can watch which way the individual you are kissing is moving his or her head, and you can turn the inverse way. It couldn't be any more obvious, in the event that you go too rapidly, you might go the say way, and afterward BAM - thumped heads. It will make it more unique on the off chance that you move all the more gradually as well.*

*Moving gradually into the kiss will likewise give you an opportunity to set you up to frame your mouth for the kiss. Try not to begin puckering when you are a foot from the other individual. When you're around five inches or somewhere in the vicinity, open your mouth marginally and pucker up a bit. It's not precisely an exemplary pucker when you are impractically kissing, it's to a greater degree a free pucker.*

## Lesson #6: Close Your Eyes

*A few individuals don't close their eyes, yet some kissing accomplices are spooked by that. So for the purpose of not running off your first kissing accomplice, simply shut your eyes when you bolt your lips. Sometime in the future, on the off chance that it makes you excessively uncomfortable, making it impossible to close your eyes, you can stand firm and simply keep them open. It's up to your kissing accomplice to manage it on the off chance that he or she doesn't care for it.*

## Lesson #7: No Need to Turn Your Head

*Uplifting news! For your first kiss, you don't have to turn your head. Really, when you turn your head, it's truly more than one kiss. You are really discharging a little when you turn your head amid a kiss. You kiss, stop a bit, turn your head and keeping kissing. That is for another lesson however.*

*You likewise don't have to utilize your tongue. That is for more experienced kissers.*

## Lesson #8: Savor the Moment and Slowly Let Go

*When you bolt your lips, appreciate the experience. You've done it! You are in your first kiss - AH! How amazing is that?*

*At the point when does it end? No compelling reason to tally. Simply hold up a little and afterward gradually move your head back a bit. Your kissing accomplice will comprehend that the kissing is over and move his or her head back as well.*

*As you move back, gradually open your head, investigate the eyes of your kissing accomplice and grin.*

*Sneak in a speedy little kiss once you isolate from the lips. It's charming and demonstrates that you truly loved the kiss. It will send an additional little shudder down his or her spine.*

*You have the information now to kiss somebody and with this learning, you have the force. Take it and use it to make a standout amongst the most significant snippets of your life. Your reasons for alarm will soon be behind you when you have your first ever kiss. You'll need to do it here and there, so it should be presently.*

*Kissing a woman out on the town or a vacant corridor is about impeccable timing. You attempt to kiss her a minute too soon, and she might step back. You attempt to kiss her a minute past the point of no return, and she might have lost the state of mind. Presently it sounds truly precarious.*

*Be that as it may, there are approaches to turn things to support you, and make the ideal science at whatever point you need!*

*The most effective method to kiss a woman .*

*The greatest stress for any fellow who needs to kiss a woman is the feared minute when you pucker up and push ahead, and she steps back! It just makes everything quite a lot more ungainly. What's more, in the event that she ever backs far from a kiss, things could simply go from clumsy to no contact! So if that you do like a woman and frantically need to kiss her, don't commit the essential error of getting the timing incorrectly.*

## *Rushing into a first kiss*

*There's no inclination that is more awful than lurching for a kiss, just to watch your date make a cumbersome expression and back her body far from you. *her humiliated grin or giggle will just make things quite a lot more awkward!* What's more, that* *would quite often happen if that you hurry into the kiss without allowing your date to set herself up for that inescapable kiss.*

*If that she enjoys you as of now, odds are, she may not restrict your kiss. Yet, in the event that it's only a first date, and you rush for a kiss, each probability she might step back regardless of the possibility that she supposes you're a decent gentleman and had examined over kissing you sooner or later during the date. [Read: How to touch a woman out on the town and warm her up for a kiss]*

*Take it moderate, utilize the strides given beneath, and you'll be well on your approach to idealizing each kiss. What's more, the best part, you'll have the capacity to utilize any situation to make the ideal setting for that first kiss, and kiss the woman regardless of the fact that she's never at any point considered kissing you yet! [Read: 11 moves to entice a woman and get her in bed inside of a couple days!]*

### *#1 Alone time.*

*The most essential thing you have to guarantee is security. Kissing a woman surprisingly is unbalanced for the initial few moments, until it begins to get great. However, for that move to be smooth, you have to keep away from any sort of diversions.*

*Attempt to get some alone time with the woman, be it in your room, in your auto after the date, or in a peaceful corner as you walk her home. It's essential that you locate the perfect spot with a considerable measure of security, or you might wind up destroying all odds of kissing her.*

### *#2 Don't discuss the kiss.*

*If that you know the woman as of now, odds are, you've talked with her about the first kiss sooner or later of time, either while content playing with her or via telephone. [Read: 20 hot inquiries to message a woman and make her wet!] In any case, when you're in the occasion, in a peaceful spot where there's nobody else however you two, don't discuss it. Try also anything about needing to kiss her or about needing to make out with her. She knows both of you have examined it thus do you. Try not to make the circumstance cumbersome by arm contorting her into a kiss in light of the fact that both of you have discussed it!*

### *#3 Take your time.*

*There's in no way such as the ideal time to kiss a woman, particularly when you're the person who's in control of the circumstance. Unwind, take a seat with her and simply discuss something. Help her vibe quiet, in light of the fact that the more agreeable she is, the more the odds of her getting a charge out of that first kiss with you. Simply play with her, and discuss something both of you did that day.*

## *#4 Don't inquire*

*as to whether you can kiss her. It's actual, young ladies cherish a knight in sparkling shield and she'll adore a gentleman who's valiant. Be that as it may, inquiring as to whether it's alright to kiss her isn't an indication of gallantry, it's an indication of cumbersomeness. Try not to inquire as to whether you can kiss her since her answer will never be to support you. If that she's truly into you, she might acknowledge to kiss you, regardless of the possibility that she feels amazed by your *bold question*. In any case, in whatever other case, you're setting yourself for a fall.*

*There's one thing you can do however, you can kiss the woman delicately on her lips, bring your face back a couple inches, investigate her eyes and inquire as to whether you can kiss her. By doing that, you're teasing her sexually, and she would say "yes", and it'll really make the first kiss significantly more private! [Read: 15 mysteries to make your first kiss a great deal more memorable]*

### #5 Get closer.

*The most ideal approach to warm her up for the first kiss is by cozying up with her. In case you're taking a seat, seat your butt closer to her so your arm can undoubtedly brush against hers. What's more, in case you're standing, move into her own space and simply stand a couple creeps far from her body.*

*The second you get into a woman's close to home space, it'll make her vibe unbalanced. In any case, don't give her a chance to clumsiness drive you off. Converse with her and play with her, and don't make it evident that you're coming closer to her. Rather, simply imagine like you came in closer automatically, and didn't understand it. [Read: How to sit alongside a woman and make her horny and wet without being obvious]*

### #6 Warm up

*the sexual strain. Touch her regularly. Utilize your finger and run it through her hair or along her arm. Compliment her as you touch her, be it about her hair, her scent or her delicate skin. If that she grins or becomes flushed when you touch her, it's a sign she enjoys what you're doing. Talk delicately in a low tone and maintain a strategic distance from any sudden developments. Whisper in her ears, and run your fingers against hers energetically. [Read: 50 charming things to say to a woman and make her become flushed before kissing her!]*

### *#7 Make your goals clear.*

*Move in close until your face is just crawls far from her face. You don't have to quit talking however, simply say something, yet as you say it, take a gander at her lips, and after that back again at her eyes. She'll know precisely what you're taking a gander at, and her psyche would be dashing generally as quick as yours may be! Wet your own lips prudently as you gaze at her *not in a dangerous lunatic sort of way*. Licking your lips intuitively sends the message crosswise over to the woman that you expect to come in for a kiss soon, and wet lips are such a great amount of better to kiss. [Read: 10 hot tips to kiss a woman enthusiastically and stimulate her]*

### *#8 The ideal time to kiss.*

*In the event that you utilize these progressions on the most proficient method to kiss a woman surprisingly, you don't generally need to stress over the ideal time to kiss her since you're the one in complete control of things. In any case, just to make the right signal, move in closer for the kiss when there's been a touch of hush for a few moments. Quit talking and don't say anything. Simply investigate her eyes, and run your fingers through her hair. If that she just glances back at you without saying anything, that is the ideal minute you've been sitting tight for!*

### *#9 Take it simple.*

*So no doubt, you've quite recently kissed the woman. Be that as it may, don't escape and demolish the occasion. When you kiss a woman surprisingly, you should be exceptionally tender and sensitive. Place your lips on hers and kiss her lips delicately. Try not to attempt to utilize your tongue too soon into the kiss. Rather, simply unwind, and attempt to appreciate the way her lips feel against yours. You have all an ideal opportunity to attempt new things later. However, until further notice, simply concentrate on kissing her delicately, and don't get pushy.*

### *#10 Don't be overenthusiastic.*

*When you kiss the woman surprisingly, don't let your hands meander too early into the kiss, or she's simply solidify up or push your hands away *and that is a horrible inclination kill!**

*As you kiss her, place your hands on her shoulders or at the edges of her arms, and simply move it tenderly at the edges of her body. Try not to attempt to move your hands over her bosoms or her stomach unless both of you have been kissing for some time.*

*Touching a woman's bosoms during the first kiss can make things clumsy. All things considered, unless you know the ideal approach to do it and make her appreciate it. A first kiss can appear to be entangled, however by utilizing these 10 stages on the most proficient method to kiss a woman interestingly, you'll be in finished control of the circumstance the entire time. Furthermore, you'll unquestionably assemble the right sort of sexual strain to ensure she appreciates that first kiss, the same amount of as you do!*

# Chapter 7

## How to prepare a woman for your bedroom

### 1. Treat her like gold

*It is basic that you generally treat a lady like gold when drowning so as to have intercourse to her in enthusiasm. By giving the session your everything without fail, you can make certain you'll gain the notoriety of a decent beau. At the point when word gets around, you can make certain that other ladies will need an essence of that zesty kielbasa. Simply recall not to do the gloating yourself; let the women (who actually love to prattle) deal with that for you.*

## *2-Always look great*

*Most ladies are fussy, materialistic and have a powerless spot for stylish men. If that you don't take an ideal opportunity to prep yourself, stay spotless and dress to inspire the women, why on the planet would they ever need to grimy their hands with you? Either play the diversion, or go play in the sandbox.*

## *3-Make ladies feel great around you*

*If that whatever you do is discuss sex when you're around ladies, then you may make some of them extremely uncomfortable. Rather, focus your discussions on different subjects, for example, your work, companions and leisure activities. The thought is to make it appear as if the keep going thing at the forefront of your thoughts is to engage in sexual relations with this specific magnificence. This works truly well in the event that she definitely realizes that you're a decent significant other (see number 1).*

## 4-Use charm

*Allure is essentially the specialty of telling somebody that you like them, without a ulterior rationale. Apply certainty, not presumptuousness. Be magnanimous. You ought not request anything consequently, not even input. Try not to be sexual, be inviting.*

## 5-Be straightforward

*The exact opposite thing you need to do is make a lady trust that you're playing with her since you're keen on a relationship. Make it clear that you're not intrigued by dating, but rather have been yearning for the organization of a "genuine" lady and that "genuine" ladies are elusive. This ought to give her an indication to ascend to the test, particularly if that she sees that you would never settle for less.*

## 6-Develop your sex offer

*Charm, certainty and cordiality emanate sex offer, however toss a decent physical make-up in with the general mish-mash and you'll have a deadly blend that'll make ladies shudder for you.*

## 7-Make her vibe hot around you

*She may feel somewhat thick around the waist, however regardless, every time you see her, she generally looks damn provocative and you generally tell her it by saying things like, "Amazing, each time I see you you're looking better and better. What's your mystery?"*

## 8-Introduce rivalry

*If that she wasn't certain about playing with you, well she would be wise to pick up the pace and decide as your worth just went up as a result of the expanded interest for your satisfying administrations. As such, don't be timid to enlighten her regarding alternate women throughout your life. Simply bear in mind to say that you're not extremely intrigued by them.*

## 9-Flirt

*Being a tease includes being certain, fun loving, fun, and puzzling. Being a tease includes your entire body — eyes (take a gander at her), hands (put your hand on her shoulder), mouth (grin), and ears (tune in). Consolidate everything and demonstrate her that you are truly keen on her.*

## 10-Use a negative hit simultaneously

*You know the amount you can't stand it when a lady lets you know, "I like you as a companion"? Well ladies despise it as well. So give them their very own little taste drug by giving her the insight that she's equitable a lot of a "decent young lady" for you to take things past the being a tease stage. Say something like, "I believe you're just excessively prudent for me."*

## 11-Tell her a story

*Uncover that you've had enough of ladies who don't know how to satisfy a man and that you've chosen to take a pledge of chastity until you meet a "genuine" lady who knows how to satisfy her mate. Trust me, most ladies will, for absence of a superior term, meet the challenge at hand.*

## 12-Tease her

*A percentage of the greatest turn-ons for ladies are reckoning, energy and the pressure got from not recognizing what's in store. Ladies love wonderful shocks. Next time, advise her you have a little astonish sitting tight for her yet you'll demonstrat to it to her one week from now.*

## 13-Kiss her

*Get some information about any lady and she'll concur that a flawless kiss will do what needs to be done. If that you stick your tongue down her throat, she'll most likely force away in repugnance. Then again, if that you kiss her delicately and gradually, then maneuver away and investigate her eyes, then kiss her again gradually and energetically — you will begin a flame within her. Remember, everything begins with a kiss.*

## open her eyes, close your mouth

*You may feel that so as to bed her, you have to persuade her how great you are sleeping, or urge her to take retribution on her sweetheart's disloyalty by having intercourse with you. However, actually she's a developed lady and as of now knows each one of those things.*

*The most ideal approach to get any lady to engage in sexual relations with you is by making all the right moves and giving her a chance to see that she's settling on the choice to lay down with you in light of what she sees (not listens) from you.*

*The fantastic Clarisse Thorn composed an awesome article in which she inquires as to why men who speak the truth about their sexual longings get discounted as dreadful (in addition to other things). It was initially posted on Alternet and it's fascinating to peruse through the remarks and contrast them with the remarks on the Jezebel repost.*

*This is okay timing for me, since I've been pondering it a great deal recently (see my posts here and here). As far as I can tell, the majority of the general population who speak and expound on male sexual vitality and how men follow up on it are ladies. While I owe a colossal obligation to the numerous ladies who offered me some assistance with shaping my comprehension and hones, I would love to see more men taking a lead around this. Thomas at Yes Means Yes is one of only a handful couple of other men I see discussing it.*

*I'm going to leave aside the men who are intentionally meddling, disagreeable, or savage. I surmise that managing them is an alternate issue than what I need to concentrate on right now since I feel that distinctive techniques are required. Rather, I need to concentrate on the folks who have great expectations, as in they would prefer not to be dreadful or obtrusive, yet wind up being seen that way.*

*Presently, I need to be clear that I understand that men tend to toss their sexual consideration around, without seeing how that can be meddlesome, intrusive and activating. Most men have no clue how dull (or more regrettable) it can be. So one part of not appearing to be frightening is showing signs of improvement comprehension of that and its effect on ladies.*

*That is a point for an alternate day. (Redesign: this post clarifies it superior to anything I ever could. Perused it and pass it on.)*

*I additionally need to be clear this isn't constrained to male-female associations. However, it is an a great deal more regular issue in those connections, both because of the ways that sexism shapes male-female connections uniquely in contrast to male-male connections, and on the grounds that men playing with or cruising men frequently do it any other way. In non-gay spaces, for instance, they are typically more inconspicuous about it since there's a chance that the gentleman you're cruising may be one of those straight folks who reacts with outrage or viciousness. Obviously, there are different complexities there, however I would prefer not to get derailed. So also, when ladies play with or voyage anybody of any sexual orientation, the progress are distinctive. Furthermore, right now, I'm discussing how men communicate with ladies.*

*One of the main motivations that a few men appear to be dreadful is that the majority of us never learn great approaches to request sex. We hear messages that let us know that it's vital to impart about sex, or that we have to ask our accomplices (or our potential accomplices) keeping in mind the end goal to get assent, yet there is next to no direction on the most proficient method to make that work. So is it any shock that there have been such a large number of men looking for counsel from get specialists and the enchantment group? Yes, a considerable measure of them are searching for approaches to control ladies. What's more, numerous others are essentially searching for the social cooperation abilities that they haven't adapted yet. So in that light, here's one approach to do it that doesn't rely on upon confusion or control. It won't work in all circumstances it's presumably best for men in previous connections, in spite of the fact that it can work in some being a tease settings.*

## 1) Let go of your connection to the result of your yearning.

*In the event that you go into the circumstance on account of a particular objective (i.e. getting laid, or getting laid specifically), you're connected to a specific result. That has a tendency to skew your activities since you're attempting to push things in a that bearing. The more you can leave things open to potential outcomes, the more space you can give you accomplice. In a world in which ladies' sexual office has a tendency to be taken away, this basic (albeit in fact regularly troublesome) step can go far to expanding her wellbeing with you. Furthermore, that makes it a great deal more probable that you'll get something that you need.*

*Remember that there is an enormous scope of sexual exercises that can be parts and heaps of fun. Quit concentrating on intercourse and find what number of different conceivable outcomes you have. They're not lesser choices. They're diverse choices, and they all check.*

*What's more, as a major aspect of that, let go of the thought that anybody other than you is in charge of your pleasure or climax. No one owes you sex. No one owes you a climax. You, and only you, are in charge of it. If that another person takes an interest in that procedure, that is dependent upon them. What's more, on the other hand, you don't owe any other individual sex or climaxes. You have the same amount of office around their goals as they have around yours.*

## *2) Start off with making it clear that you're requesting her assent.*

*Asking somebody "would you like to engage in sexual relations?" might seem like you're making space for assent. In any case, you have to recollect that we live in a world that tells numerous ladies that they can't say no. In the event that you truly need to have her assent, and you need her to trust that, have a go at beginning off with something such as:*

## *In case you're feeling horny...*

*These sorts of expressions do two things. To start with, they let her realize that you're putting forth her a probability as opposed to making an interest. They welcome and oblige her to put forth a positive expression, while making space for her to say no. Second, they advise you that she has the same amount of space to say yes or no as you do. This will can offer you some assistance with managing and contain your sexual vitality until you get a reasonable explanation of assent from her. Furthermore, that is something to be thankful for to hone.*

## *3) Follow up with an announcement of your longing.*

*I might want to engage in sexual relations with you.*

*I'm in the state of mind for a sensual caress.*

*I'd affection to tie you up.*

*it would turn me on in the event that we attempted that new vibrator.*

*I'd appreciate kissing you.*

*By putting forth a reasonable expression of your hobbies or wishes at that point, you're giving her a thought of what you need. Be straightforward and direct-don't request something you think she'll say yes to, while trusting you can take it encourage once things begin. In the event that you experience issues requesting what you need, hone it when only you're at some point. Discover the words that are real to you and think of expressions that vibe more regular when you say them.*

*When you straightforwardly and unmistakably express your goals, when you can claim them, you are talking from a position of force and quality. This is a noteworthy movement on the grounds that the vast majority of us really feel weak around sex. We're taught that ladies are the watchmen and men need to ask, pay off, persuade, or constrain them into doing what we need. When we feel frail, we regularly slip into examples of lack of involvement (which can prompt aloof animosity) or brutality. When we find our energy, we can relinquish both of those and be solid.*

## 4) Be prepared to discuss what comes next.

*Since you've relinquished your connection to the result, you'll have the capacity to let this begin a discussion about what you every need to do. If that she's not in the state of mind for A, shouldn't something be said about B, C, D, or E? Furthermore, in the event that she's simply not into engaging in sexual relations right then, you could choose to hold up until later, jack off, or (in the event that it fits inside of your relationship understandings) discover another person to inquire. All flawlessly fine alternatives.*

## 5) Practice

*Adapting better approaches to discuss sex can appear to be truly troublesome at first. We don't have numerous good examples for it and a great deal of men have disguised disgrace around sexual longings and/or discussing them. You could rehearse with one another at some point, which gives you the chance to let each know other if any expressions are particularly great or especially trying for you. What's more, obviously, you could approach her to work on approaching you for sex, utilizing this system or something else. It would give you every some more profound knowledge into alternate's encounters.*

# Chapter 8

## Steps to be taken in the bed room

*A fundamental aide for how to engage in sexual relations and how to make it great, particularly surprisingly. It ought to feel decent, not excruciating or uncomfortable. Individuals say that first time sex with somebody is dependably trash or excruciating – hogwash.*

*First time sex ought to feel okay particularly in the event that you know the sort of sex you both need to have, on the off chance that you feel great together and you can convey.*

*Would you like to isn't that right?*

*Keep in mind that the main reason justifiable reason motivation to have intercourse is that you really need to do it. You're not doing it for any other person, or to substantiate yourself, or to say you've done it, or to demonstrat to you adore somebody and so forth and so on. More about this here.*

*What is "it?"*

*Individuals regularly think they realize what 'engaging in sexual relations' implies, in any case they don't. Individuals are distinctive and they have diverse thoughts regarding what sex they might need to have. In the event that you depend on 'what considers' sex you might wind up abhorring it or notwithstanding engaging in sexual relations you haven't really consented to. So attempt to consider this before you do it and attempt to convey this to your accomplice. More help with this here and here.*

## *Take as much time as necessary*

*It's essential to require your investment for first time sex, yes to 'make it uncommon', additionally to ensure that you both have enough time to get settled, get turned on and to really appreciate it. Quick ones can be fun, yet presumably not for first time sex. I realize that youngsters don't get that much private time where they can be distant from everyone else, except attempt and give yourself several hours. Attempt to give yourselves two or three hours so you have enough time to get used to one another and to get over how weird it may feel at first.*

*Sex ought to never feel excruciating by any stretch of the imagination – on the off chance that it is please both stop. Be that as it may it may feel a tad bit abnormal at first and there's a ton to get used to. Bringing dresses off with somebody, touching somebody and having somebody touching you surprisingly can all vibe truly abnormal at first. So it's great to have a touch of time to get accustomed to it and to have the capacity to discuss how it's inclination.*

## Locate the correct spot

*You won't not have your own place or have enough money for a lodging room, so discovering some place to do it can be precarious. In any case you ought to be inside, in a private space where you can close the entryway. It ought to simply be you two and you realize that nobody will intrude.*

*Keeping in mind the end goal to appreciate sex you should be casual and agreeable and not agonizing over being intruded. Once in a while folks or carers will permit their children to do it in their home, or may 'choose not to see' on the off chance that they go out for a night, or they may not. Recall that it can be troublesome for folks to manage this:*

*what might you do on the off chance that you were a guardian of an adolescent?*

*On the off chance that you aren't generally feeling it then don't do it! Both individuals should be turned on and loose for sex to be great. Needing sex and being turned on aren't the same thing – as should be obvious here.*

*Whatever bits you have in your jeans, they ought to be throbbing.*

*Vaginas will for the most part be entirely wet; on the off chance that it isn't then the sex might feel difficult, particularly if the vaginal crown is tight. The vagina extends and unwinds when sexually stirred (turned on), this implies fingers, a sex toy or a penis ought to slide in without it harming. This is the reason it's imperative to get truly turned on first with stroking, snacking, kissing, holding, is critical. Click here for additional about the clitoris and vagina.*

*For additional wetness utilize some water based oil: for butt-centric sex or sex with toys, use heaps of it (the rear-end doesn't react to sexual excitement similarly as the vagina does). Water based lube is sheltered to use with condoms.*

*Penises get hard when turned on yet not generally. It can be difficult to get a hard on some of the time: nerves, pre-sex pressure, stresses ('will they like it', 'this is the first occasion when anybody has seen my hard on', 'will their guardians be back soon' and so forth) can all genuinely influence the hardness of a penis. Once an erection arrives it can soon leave as well. Recollect that you needn't bother with an erect penis to appreciate sex – you truly don't. Once in a while men and ladies engage in sexual relations with one another, which is well mainstream however not for everybody. When they do they can here and there find that there is a distinction between how rapidly it takes for them to get stirred. I clarify why that is here.*

## *Romantic affair*

*They make passage sex (vaginal or butt-centric sex) look dead simple in movies – one individual gets in the middle of the legs of the other and effectively slides into them – however it's not as simple as it looks. In case you're doing it interestingly then it's a smart thought to jerk off one another for somewhat first. You could likewise embed a wet, finger inside your accomplice first. Do this gradually and deliberately. At the point when your accomplice is more casual you can move your finger around and after that embed another finger. This makes the opening sufficiently huge to embed a penis or toy. It causes for other individual to control their accomplice to the correct spot.*

*"*

*In case you're going to have passage sex you have to go truly gradually and deliberately at first. Nothing ought to be "constrained." At that point put the hard penis (inside a condom) or toy inside, gradually at first. Gradually. Continue checking in with one another this feels alright. On the off chance that it does then you can steadily develop the rate and hardness in the event that you need. Once the penis is sliding in and out effectively you can choose to move all the more rapidly and hard, or do it gradually and profoundly.*

## *The "best" position*

*As I would see it individuals are somewhat fixated on the right position for sex. Finding the right position relies on upon what you both like, how versatile you are and what sort of sex you need. There are no principles and no enchantment positions: simply do what feels great. In case you're doing it interestingly it may be best to pick a position where you are both confronting one another. Correspondence (both with or without words) is simpler when you can see every others faces. More on positions here.*

## *Conveying*

*In the event that you've discussed the sort of sex you need to do and don't have any desire to do then you might have a thought of what's in store. However in the event that things begin feeling uncomfortable or not what you expected then you ought to both stop. During sex it's critical to truly pay consideration on whether one another are getting a charge out of it.*

*You can utilize words and short expressions (which are frequently less demanding to exclaim) whilst you're doing it. You can likewise convey through different commotions, outward appearances and the way we touch one another.*

## Orgasm

*In movies, TV, porn and books (taking a gander at you Fifty Shades) everybody has climaxes truly effortlessly. Climaxes can feel extraordinary amid sex, however not everybody has them when they engage in sexual relations with somebody. Distinctive individuals need various types of sex and touch to have climaxes. Case in point penis in vagina sex is normally more fortifying for the penis than the vagina. Likewise it can be troublesome for individuals to 'let go' amid sex and have one. Likewise when you truly need something it can make it harder – you know when you truly need to get the chance to rest yet can't? So attempt and chill, take the weight off and simply feel what feels decent.*

*On the off chance that you do the greater part of this, with somebody you like and trust, then sex can feel really stunning. How incredible sex feels is hard to say however here and there it feels pleasant, ameliorating, personal. Here and there it feels energizing, invigorating, energetic, knee trembling. At times both! In the event that it feels awful, sickening, frightening badly, dangerous, exhausting, simply something you are doing in light of the fact that you think you should: then why are you doing it.*

*Engaging in sexual relations can be a considerable measure of fun and extremely fulfilling, however that being said in the event that you are in regards to attempt it interestingly and don't know where to begin. Here's a manual for help you unravel that sexual code — a regulated aide on the most proficient method to have intercourse.*

## *Step #1:*

*Find out if the individual needs to engage in sexual relations: This is the most critical part around a decent sexual ordeal. On the off chance that one of the accomplices is not 'in the state of mind' or would not like to have intercourse it can prompt the whole process going bad. Also the way that it can abandon you or your accomplice with a feeling of being disregarded or utilized. Along these lines, see whether he/she needs to engage in sexual relations. Some basic pointers you ought to pay special mind to is if the individual appears to be enthused about being with you physically, touches you or builds his/her closeness to you. In spite of the fact that these are signs, please recall that you should not misread the signs and now and then asking is the most ideal approach to know. Here is an orderly manual for get your lady in inclination for sex.*

## Step #2:

*Be arranged: Sex is a great thing. It's pleasurable and fulfills you feel. It additionally has various other medical advantages like offering you some assistance with burning calories and beating gloom. It's no big surprise that we are the main species that has intercourse for joy and not exclusively multiplication. Yet, with all that fun come issues like undesirable pregnancies, STDs and enthusiastic mishaps. So being readied is your best alternative. Convey a condom, have that preventative pill and recollect that you should be rationally prepared for the demonstration. Sex brings individuals closer. That is only the way people are naturally made. So on the off chance that you are wanting to have an one-night stand or are making the first stride towards a submitted relationship recall that you ought to have your brain in a state of harmony with what your body needs. One great approach to do this is to discuss it. Inquire as to whether they have insurance (on the off chance that you don't, go out and purchase a few, there are a great deal of alternatives to look over), converse with him/her about what you trust this could prompt and in particular speak the truth about how you see the demonstration (whether it is something you simply need to accomplish for delight without any strings appended or something more genuine.). Keep in mind, condoms are set aside a few minutes use. You can't utilize one condom over and over so ensure you purchase enough, just on the off chance that you plan to go at it more than once. Perused more around 5 motivations to have intercourse at this moment!*

## *Step #3:*

*Choose the area and set the mind-set: Sex is a personal demonstration, at any rate it ought to be. So pick a spot where both of you will be uninhibited, particularly in the event that it's your first time. Pick a spot that is private and has an agreeable spot to have intercourse in. A decent delicate bed with mind-set lighting dependably helps the reason (unless you plan to tread on a trial way). So overdo it a smidgen. Keep in mind delight comes at an expense. Here are 11 melodies to get you in the disposition for sex.*

## *Step #4:*

*Approach the individual delicately and don't appear to be excessively edgy: Coming on too unequivocally or being pushy about having intercourse is one of the greatest mood killers. So don't appear to be frantic (regardless of the fact that you are passing on to be with the individual), permit the other individual some space to express their sentiments too. You should demonstrate that you are occupied with getting physically private however back off on the off chance that you feel the other individual is not responding. Sex ought to be a decision so given them a chance to pick. In the event that you two are sufficiently close you could basically ask him/her. It will be a danger worth taking. Here are 7 tips to get your fantasy lady to adore you!*

## *Step #5:*

*Kiss and touch: The initial move towards physical closeness is kissing. Most ladies affection to kiss and an enthusiastic kiss can place her in the temperament for some more. In addition being close, kissing, touching and stroking your accomplice invigorates their erogenous zones which will prompt more pleasurable sex. It additionally prompts a more grounded feeling of closeness and wellbeing – two feelings that offer a man some assistance with performing better in bed. So touch him/her, kiss and make your accomplice needed. This is likewise another approach to control the individual's self-perception issues (in the event that they have any), making them more agreeable in your vicinity. Here's a regulated manual for kiss a young lady.*

## Step# 6:

*Have a considerable measure of foreplay: This is the place you can either uproot your garments or have your accomplice strip you. Another approach to take is to uproot one bit of attire at once, making the whole process a secret. With regards to foreplay, a great many people imagine that sex is just penetrative. However, the demonstration includes foreplay. Foreplay, as the name proposes is your main thing before you have intercourse. It incorporates petting, kissing, empowering your accomplice's erogenous zones and oral sex too. Ensure you get enough of this in. It is frequently the most pleasant part of the entire sexual experience on the grounds that you two can explore different avenues regarding various routines. Tip for men: Women can climax different times. So delight your lady, she will be in the inclination for some more and thank you for it in a greater number of courses than one. Tip for ladies: Most men adoration to be touched also, so make him feel great. Touch him, kiss him and feel his whole body. Try not to keep down and don't be the stand out hoarding all the joy. Here are 5 foreplay tips to supercharge your sexual coexistence.*

## *Step#7:*

*Pick the right minute: The right minute to have penetrative sex is normally felt and is frequently shared. Pick the minute when your accomplice truly needs to proceed onward to the following step. At times inquiring as to whether the other individual is prepared or on the off chance that he/she needs more is a decent approach to know when now is the ideal time. When you realize that he/she is prepared, take it to the following level. Perused more about What's the best time to have intercourse?*

## *Step #7a:*

*Insertion: This is the most advertised part about sex and is regularly accepted to be the main thing that happens amid it. In any case, there's nothing further from reality. In this stride the penis is embedded into the vagina. Tip for men: The vagina is a flexible organ display just underneath the lady's vulva (outside lips of her privates). On the off chance that you are having defensive sex, ensure you wear a condom before you embed your penis into her vagina. Various men get the position wrong and tend to 'glance around' with their penis (attempt to enter without knowing where the vagina is) this can be excruciating for the lady. So a decent approach to discover the vagina without being humiliated is to request that your accomplice help you. Here are 10 approaches to give your lady different climaxes*

## *Step#8:*

*Love making: Once the introductory entrance is finished, you can engage in sexual relations anyway you both are agreeable. Men, ensure you push (your penis into her vagina) in musical movements and do it from the hip; this will guarantee your lady gets the most extreme joy. Moving your whole body is counterproductive. In particular listen to your accomplice and your body. Permit yourself to feel delight and ensure you think about your accomplice's pleasure and make her cheerful as well. Tip for ladies: Be proactive in bed. Move when your man moves. Pushing can be pleasurable and significantly all the more so when you both are doing it in a state of harmony and together. Tell your man what you do and don't care for. Make beyond any doubt you delight him also. Nobody likes somebody who hoards all the delight for themselves. For the women, here's ladies' manual for first-time sex.*

## *Step #9:*

*Last couple of minutes: Once you both have peaked or the sex is going to get over, you both will most presumably be in a condition of rapture. Permit yourselves to be in that state for whatever length of time that you should be. Keep in mind this is the stage where you can hold one another or essentially be alongside one another. Try not to surge things; let your body return to its typical state. Hurried sex can be energizing here and there however in the event that it is done all the time it can abandon you feeling somewhat fragmented. Tip for men: Most ladies like to be held or nestled as of right now. Humor her. After the sum total of what she has been an accomplice in your sexual frolic. Tip for ladies: If you enjoyed the experience, tell your accomplice that. There is in no way such as a sense of self support after a decent time between the sheets.*

## *Step #10:*

*Winding up: The post coital part can be flawless at times and ungainly in others. So attempt to make your accomplice agreeable. Give him/her a shirt to wear, be a tease a little and let him know/her how great the experience was. Grin and share a giggle together. This could be the best time to make a decent companion or an accomplice forever. So utilize the open door. After you'll are done, ensure you'll clean up. Ladies, wash your vaginal opening and vulva and men ought to wash their penis once they evacuate the condom. Finally, ensure you discard the condom legitimately. Try not to flush it down the latrine. Toss it in a dustbin wrapped in paper or tissue paper.*

# Chapter 9

## How to execute first kiss

### 1-Kiss her energetically

*I'm certain you've kissed your lady a lot of times, yet have you kissed her so enthusiastically that her clothing just mystically falls off? Whenever you need to begin things up, container her face in your grasp, look in her eyes for two seconds, and after that kiss her.*

*While you're kissing her, don't push your tongue down her throat whenever. Occasionally lick her lips and knead her tongue with your own. Too, move your hands to the back of her hair and take hold of it solidly from the roots.*

*Continue kissing her, however gradually move your hands around her body with a specific end goal to give her a chance to encounter diverse sensations at the same time. In any case, don't touch her bosoms or vagina just yet.*

## 2-Remove her top gradually

*Removing her garments is a turn-on for both of you. Be that as it may, when you disrobe your lady, don't rip off her garments — save that savage conduct for one more day. Today, you're going to gradually unfasten her shirt (on the off chance that she's not wearing a catch out, then lift the top over her head and evacuate it), however abandon her bra on.*

*Work your mouth around the edges of her bra and kiss her bosoms from the top and the sides. Too, gently run your fingertips over her ribcage and waist.*

*When you're prepared to remove that bra, let your mouth skim over her areolas, however don't outrightly suck or lick them.*

*Your goal is to tease her, and this is only the starting...*

## 3-Massage her delicately

*After you've evacuated her shirt and bra, kiss her as you did some time recently, however this time, work your hands in the face of her good faith and tap your fingertips here and there on it. As your kiss increments in its forcefulness, so too ought to the back rub you're giving.*

*Utilize your hands to work her over from the base to the top and withdraw once more. At that point, work your hands up her sides and advance down to her butt. On the off chance that you can, get your hands down to her external thighs, lift her up and wrap her legs around your waist.*

*Advance toward an area where you can lay her down.*

## 4-Sex her dryly

*Leaving your jeans on (and hers as well), put her down and gradually put your body over hers. Next, start copying the movements you'd experience on the off chance that you were infiltrating her. This is to get her creative energy and juices streaming.*

*Once more, kiss her tenderly, put your hands under her shoulders and clutch them as you push like you're advancing inside her. In case you're erect, all the better. She'll feel your strong part and envision what's coming next.*

## 5-Undress her unobtrusively

*Presently it's an ideal opportunity to take everything off. Each time you evacuate a thing of her attire, kiss and lick that body part.*

*What's more, don't race through the disrobing process; take as much time as necessary and make a point to demonstrate her that you value her body. When you're set, disrobe yourself gradually and lay by her.*

## 6-Rub her teasingly

*Oral sex is dependably a choice when you're exposed with your lady, yet this evening, maybe you'd be ideally serviced by teasing your lady in an unexpected way. After you slip on your condom, apply some lube and rub your penis gradually here and there her vulva.*

*Let just the leader of your penis slide in "unintentionally," then uproot it and keep rubbing her labia and clitoris. When she at long last starts to beseech you to get inside, the foreplay closes and the finale start.*

# Chapter 10

## Basic Sex Positions

## 1. Five Yoga Sex Positions to Help Your Sex Life

*Attempt these simple yoga breathing positions to get you started...in a bigger number of routes than one!*

## 2. The Reverse Cowgirl Position

*Maybe one of the more mainstream sex positions, with the Reverse Cowgirl the point of the penis through the front mass of the vagina fortifies the territory of her G-spot. She'll cheerful thus will you. Cowgirl cap not required, but rather very recommended.*

## 3. Heels to the Sky Position

*Will "sex noticeable all around" truly make for the best sex position? One fellow thinks in this way, so perhaps give it a spin.*

## 4. The Yab-Yum Position

*Begin confronting one another - in the Yab-Yum position, which is you leg over leg and her sitting in your lap confronting you, by and large with our temples touching. At that point, synchronize your relaxing. Goodness, and there's additional. Good fortunes.*

## 5. The Finger Sex Position

*How about we take it straightforward. Outdated tips and traps on the best way to finger a young lady gained from the Japanese by twisting your list and center fingers like you're holding the trigger of a M1 carbine and apply consistent, cadenced weight simply inside the vagina.*

# Chapter 11

## Something you should avoid during sex

### 1. NOT KISSING FIRST

*Keeping away from her lips and plunging straight for the erogenous zones makes her vibe like you're paying by the hour and cutting so as to attempt to get your cash's worth out unnecessary items. A legitimate energetic kiss is a definitive type of foreplay.*

### 2. BLOWING TOO HARD IN HER EAR.

*Let it out, some child at school let you know young ladies cherish this. All things considered, there's a distinction between being sexual and blowing as though you're attempting to smother the candles on*

*your 50th birthday cake. That damages.*

### 3. NOT SHAVING

*You frequently overlook you have a porcupine strapped to your button which you rake more than once over your accomplice's face and thighs. When she turns her head from side to side, it's not energy, it's shirking.*

## 4. Pressing HER BREAST.

*Most men act like a housewife testing a melon for readiness when they get their hand on a couple. Stroke, touch, and smooth them.*

## 5. Gnawing HER NIPPLES.

*Why do men attach onto a lady's areolas, then clasp down like they're attempting to flatten her body by means of her bosoms? Areolas are exceptionally delicate. They can't stand up to biting. Lick and suck them tenderly. Flicking your tongue crosswise over them is great. Imagining they're a doggie toy isn't.*

## 6. TWIDDLING HER NIPPLES.

*Quit doing that thing where you twiddle the areolas in the middle of finger and thumb like you're attempting to locate a radio station in an uneven zone. Concentrate in general bosoms, not only the shout focuses.*

## 7. Disregarding THE OTHER PARTS OF HER BODY

*A lady is not a parkway with only three side roads: Breastville East and West, and the Midtown Tunnel. There are inconceivable territories of her body which you've disregarded far again and again as you go bombarding straight into downtown Vagina. So begin paying them some consideration.*

## 8. GETTING THE HAND TRAPPED.

*Poor manual skill in the underskirt area can bring about tangled fingers and underpants. In case will be that forceful, simply request that her take the damn things off.*

## 9) LEAVING HER A LITTLE PRESENT

*Condom transfer is the man's obligation. You wore it you store it.*

## 10) ATTACKING THE CLITORIS

*Direct weight is extremely offensive, so tenderly pivot your fingers nearby of the clitoris.*

## 11) STOPPING FOR A BREAK

*Ladies, not at all like men, don't get where they cleared out off. In the event that you stop, they fall*

*starting over from the beginning quick. In the event that you can tell she's not there, continue going by any stretch of the imagination costs numb jaw or not.*

## 12) UNDRESSING HER AWKWARDLY

*Ladies loathe looking inept, yet imbecilic she will look when stripped at the waist with a sweater stuck over her head. Unwrap her like an exquisite present, not a child's toy.*

## 13) GIVING HER A WEDGIE DURING FOREPLAY.

*Stroking her tenderly through her underwear can be exceptionally attractive Pulling the material up between her thighs and yanking it forward and backward is definitely not.*

## 14) BEING OBSESSED WITH THE VAGINA

*Although most men can discover the clitoris without maps despite everything they trust that the*

*vagina is the place it's all at. No sooner is your hand down there than you're attempting to stuff stolen banknotes up a smokestack. This is alright on a basic level, yet in the event that you're not watchful, it can hurt - so don't escape. It's best to pay more regard for her clitoris and the outside of her vagina at in the first place, then tenderly slip a finger inside her and check whether she loves it.*

## 15) MASSAGING TOO ROUGHLY

*You're endeavoring to give her an exotic, unwinding back rub to get her in the state of mind.*

*Hands and fingertips are alright elbows and knees are most certainly not.*

## 16) UNDRESSING PREMATURELY

*Try not to constrain the issue by stripping before she's at any rate made some move toward getting your stuff off, regardless of the fact that it's simply fixing several catches.*

## 17) TAKING YOUR PANTS OFF FIRST

*A man in socks and underpants is an even from a pessimistic standpoint. Lose the socks first.*

## 18) GOING TOO FAST

*When you get to the penis-in-vagina circumstance, the most exceedingly terrible thing you can do is*

*pump away like a modern force instrument - she'll soon feel like a get together - line laborer made out of date by your innovation. Develop gradually, with clean straight, consistent pushes.*

## 19) GOING TOO HARD

*In the event that you bash your incredible triangular hip bones into her thigh or stomach, the torment is equivalent to two weeks of horseback riding gathered into a few moments.*

## 20) COMING TOO SOON

*Each man's apprehension. With reason. On the off chance that you shoot before you see the whites of her eyes, ensure you have a reinforcement plan to guarantee her pleasure as well.*

## 21) NOT COMING SOON ENOUGH

*It might appear to you that bumping for 60 minutes without peaking is the characteristic of a sex god, however to her it's more probable the sign of an unresponsive vagina. At any rate purchase some fascinating inside decorations, so she has something to hold her advantage while you're playing Marathon Man.*

## 22) ASKING IF SHE HAS COME

*You truly should have the capacity to tell. Most ladies make clamor. However, in the event that you truly*

*don't have the foggiest idea, don't inquire.*

## 23) PERFORMING ORAL SEX TOO GENTLY

*Try not to act such as a monster feline at a saucer of milk. Get your entire mouth down there,*

*furthermore, focus on tenderly turning or flicking your tongue on her clitoris.*

## 24) NUDGING HER HEAD DOWN

*Men hold on in doing this until she's eyeball-to-penis trusting that it will lead swiftly to mouth-to-penis. All ladies despise this. It's around three stages from being dragged to a hollow by their hair. In the event that you need her to utilize her mouth, use yours; have a go at talking alluringly to her.*

## 25) NOT WARNING HER BEFORE YOU CLIMAX

*Sperm possesses a flavor like ocean water blended with egg white. Not everyone likes it. At the point when she's performing oral sex, caution her before you come so she can do what's vital.*

## 26) MOVING AROUND DURING FELLATIO

*Try not to push. She'll do all the moving amid fellatio You simply lie there. What's more, try not to snatch her head.*

## 27) TAKING ETIQUETTE ADVICE FROM PORN MOVIES

*In X-appraised motion pictures, ladies appear to cherish it when men discharge over them. In genuine*

*life, it just means more clothing to do.*

## 28) MAKING HER RIDE ON TOP FOR AGES.

*Requesting that her be on top is fine. Lying there snorting while she does all the diligent work is definitely not. Stroke her tenderly, with the goal that she doesn't feel so much like the skipper of a clipper. What's more, given her a chance to have a rest.*

## *29) ATTEMPTING ANAL SEX AND PRETENDING IT WAS AN ACCIDENT*

*This is the manner by which men procure a notoriety for not having the capacity to take after headings. In the event that you need to put it there, ask her first. Also, don't surmise that being tipsy is an pardon.*

## *30) TAKING PICTURES*

*At the point when a man says, "Would I be able to take a photograph of you?" she'll hear the words "to appear my amigos." At minimum let her have care of them.*

## *31) NOT BEING IMAGINATIVE ENOUGH*

*Creative energy is anything from stepping designs on her back to pouring nectar on her and licking it off. Organic product, vegetables, ice and plumes are all helpful props; hot flame wax and changeless color are a no.*

## *32) SLAPPING YOUR STOMACH AGAINST HERS.*

*There is no less sexual commotion. It's as provocative as a burping challenge.*

## 33) ARRANGING HER IN STUPID POSES.

*On the off chance that she needs to do propelled yoga in bed, fine, yet unless she's a Romanian athlete, don't get excessively aspiring. Inquire as to whether you need a sexual accomplice with snapped hamstrings.*

## 34) LOOKING FOR HER PROSTATE

*Perused this painstakingly: Anal incitement feels useful for men since they have a prostate. Ladies don't.*

## 35) GIVING LOVE BITES.

*It is very sexual to apply some tender suction on the sides of the neck, if you do it painstakingly. No lady needs to need to wear turtlenecks and dapper Scarves for a considerable length of time.*

## 36) BARKING INSTRUCTIONS.

*Try not to yell support like a mentor with a bull horn It's not a major turn-on.*

## 37) TALKING DIRTY.

*It makes you seem like a desolate magazine proofreader calling a 1-900 line. On the off chance that she*

*likes awful talk, she'll tell you.*

## 38) NOT CARING WHETHER SHE COMES.

*You need to complete the employment. Continue attempting until you hit the nail on the head, and she may indeed, even do likewise for you.*

### *39) SQUASHING HER.*

*Men for the most part measure more than ladies, so in the event that you lie on her a bit too vigorously, she will turn blue.*

### *40) THANKING HER.*

*Never thank a lady for having intercourse with you. Your room is not a soup kitchen.*

# Chapter 12

## Some don’ts after sexual activity

*- 14 things to avoid If this is an one night stand, then you ought to likely be acting uniquely in contrast to after sex with your spouse of ten years, however in both circumstances it's about being chivalrous of how your man feels, while not overlooking your own needs.*

*At any rate this is what not to do (and how that may apply in whatever circumstance you're in).*

### *Approaching How It Was For her*

*With a new mate, don't approach how it was for her or fish for compliments. It makes you look unstable. She may let you know the amount she appreciated it without you inquiring as to whether it was that great, it will most likely be evident and words are not required. In the event that you had a decent time, expect she did as well. On the off chance that you need to ask, you may be putting her in an unbalanced position of lying to save your emotions. Either that or you will be harmed on the off chance that she is not exactly complimentary.*

*With a long haul accomplice, in case you're developing enough to regard fair replies, ask anything you like, particularly in the event that you simply took a stab at something new. It's the best approach to enhance your sexual coexistence – however regardless you shouldn't have to angle for compliments – only data about what she prefers.*

## Looking at her

*Any sort of examination with another lady or notice of any past partner after you engaged in sexual relations is a finished No – it doesn't make a difference on the off chance that you've known tshe fellow five minutes or a quarter century. Try not to do it!*

*Getting Immediately On With Your Life*

*You're occupied. She's occupied. In any case, unless you both comprehended this was a fast in and out and that you had only a brief span before you needed to accomplish something else, it's terrible conduct just to engage in sexual relations then open your book, switch on the TV or begin taking a gander at your cell phone or tablet to check whether you have any messages. A little discussion and warmth/benevolence never hurt anybody!*

*With another accomplice, requesting that she leave since you have things to do immediately, regardless of the possibility that you never need to see her again, will make her feel objectified and that you just scratched a tingle instead of engaged in sexual relations with a living, person. Try not to be a bitch – save his sentiments somewhat, regardless of the fact that you never go out with her again or call her after she in the long run takes off.*

## *Separating Yourself*

*Regardless of the fact that you don't move on immediately, you can be generally as far off in your mind by physically moving separated and considering something/somebody other than your significant other even while you are still in bed with her. Concentrate on the fellow for a bit regardless of to what extent you've known her. It won't slaughter you to be thoughtful or cherishing.*

## Washing Her Away

*On the off chance that you jump out of bed quickly after sex and give the feeling that you detest the thought that she ever touched you, it can feel extremely unsettling to your gentleman. A long-standing accomplice might be utilized to it, however most likely still doesn't care for the way you do that. A fast nestle before tidy up is all it takes to make this appear to be less pernicious. See Washing after sex for additional on the behavior behind getting clean in the wake of having intercourse.*

## Brushing Your Teeth

*Brushing your teeth or utilizing mouth wash directly after sex is like washing and won't charm you to your new significant other or accomplice either. In the event that you had oral sex, living with the taste a while longer is not going to slaughter you.*

## Sickening Her

*It should abandon saying that you ought to maintain a strategic distance from any of the real mood killers with any sweetheart such as nose picking, burping, fluctuating, ass scratching, picking your nails and so forth. Be that as it may, in the event of some unforeseen issue, I included it for fulfillment...*

## *Nodding off*

*You may feel exceptionally drowsy in tshe wake of coming to climax, that is fine yet don't go right to rest without a little discussion or closeness. It's simply awful behavior. Presently she might go right to consider you yet that is anotsher story. See Cuddling After Making Love for additional on this.*

## *Pronouncing Your Love*

*With a built up accomplice saying "I Love You" after sex is an awesome approach to affirm your thankfulness and fondness. With another accomplice it may set alerts ringing and make them keep running for the slopes. In a perfect world you need the "I adore you" minute to happen surprisingly outside the room during a period when you are both unaffected by the glimmer of good sex.*

## *Requesting Commitment*

*It's pretty much as critical not to inquire as to whether she adores you as it is not to pronounce your adoration for her directly after sex in a moderately new relationship. Same inquiring as to whether she need to be your sweetheart/selective/you to move in with her. Every one of these discussions ought to happen suddenly outside the room else they appear as though they are a desire since you engaged in sexual relations.*

## Being Eager For More Action Too Soon

*Your gentleman needs a recuperation period in the wake of having intercourse. The more established she is, the more extended the recuperation period she's going to require. Try not to grasp his bundle seeking after all the more directly after sex. She's not going to appreciate that, particularly on the off chance that she knows there's no chance at any point in the near future. Nestle up and see what falls into place without a hitch. On the off chance that you didn't climax it's Ok to request that she complete you off – it's something she ought to be doing as opposed to leaving you without a friend in tshe world at any rate.*

## Crying

*Try not to cry unless you need to unnerve her stupid. Folks abhor a lot of feeling and tears. With another accomplice, odds are you'll never see her again. You ought to get more understanding from a long haul accomplice on the other hand, however regardless she won't care for it.*

## Staying nearby Too Long

*With another significant other don't exceed your welcome. When you get up in the morning, get a taxi and leave with your nobility in place. Leave your number on the off chance that you'd like her to call. Staying longer won't make her any more prone to call. Obviously, on the off chance that she requests that you stay a bit, and you need to, that is an alternate matter!*

### Snickering

*You'll blow a gasket another beau by chuckling or laughing directly after sex. She'll ponder what you are snickering at. Her? His penis? His procedure? Giggling is presumably not very savvy with a long standing significant other either, unless she knows you so well she knows precisely why you are chuckling and is totally ok with it.*

# Chapter 13

## Natural herbs for erectile dysfunction

*Men have constantly endeavored to help their "execution" or masculinity by searching for a characteristic solution for erectile dysfunction (ED). Every last culture has imagined an ED cure, from eating bulls' testicles to shark blade soup. Best case scenario, normal cures will contain the same fixing as Viagra, however in much lower amounts, which makes them essentially less powerful.*

*The force of the psyche is not to be thought little of with regards to having faith in cures so they might some of the time work, regardless of the fact that they don't contain any dynamic substance (this is known as a misleading impact). Be that as it may, home grown ED cures offered online can show real wellbeing dangers. It is imperative that you comprehend your treatment alternatives before you take any prescription.*

*Underneath, we elucidate the dangers and threats of taking home grown Viagra, and clarify your treatment alternatives.*

*Is there a protected option treatment for erectile dysfunction?*

*Numerous conventional cures are being sold on the web, because of the uncommon interest for ED medicines.*

*This is stressing in light of the way that only 1 in 4 men will talk about their ED with an expert specialist, as it recommends that numerous are buying so as to take a chance with their wellbeing questionable items on the web. As a rule, ED is brought on by a basic cardiovascular issue, which requires prompt treatment. Ensure you converse with an expert. This can be up close and personal, or on the off chance that you feel excessively humiliated, you can counsel our online specialist.*

*What Are The Dangers Of Unregulated Herbal Viagra?*

*Numerous option cures have not been authorized and tried. At times, venders have changed the equation, bundling and naming to stay away from administrative issues. National organizations which direct pharmaceuticals and online drug stores need to manage an inconceivable number of new medicines offered, and numerous inadequate or perilous medications wind up available. Unregulated medications might contain an off base measurement or a hurtful substance.*

*In the UK, legitimate home grown cures indicate either the THR (customary natural enlistment) logo or the item permit on the mark.*

*What Are The Alternative Treatments?*

*At the point when searching for a characteristic cure for erectile dysfunction, your indexed lists on the web may demonstrate entirely confounding. You'll take a gander at an interminable rundown, every item asserting to be the best or most old et cetera. Specialists have figured out how to separate these medications into a short rundown, taking into account the dynamic guideline behind each of these natural cures.*

## *DHEA*

*DHEA is a steroid hormone normally delivered by the body; it just aides when you have a low level of testosterone, which is an uncommon condition and unrealistic to bring about ED.*

*Symptoms incorporate skin break out and a decreased level of good cholesterol. Large amounts of awful cholesterol can after some time lead to ED.*

## Horny Goat Weed

*Late research demonstrates, that this old chinese cure works in a comparable manner as Viagra. Under the name of a characteristic cure for erectile dysfunction, horny goat weed is presumably the most popular treatment accessible on the web.*

*On the other hand, its impact is by and large 80 times not as much as Viagra, so accomplishing a viable measurement is troublesome.*

## Vitamins

*A few supplements and vitamins are here and there publicized as solutions for erectile dysfunction, as well. In men with a zinc inadequacy, taking a zinc supplement will cause yet you have to be careful with taking an overdose. Too high a level of zinc in your body can hurt your invulnerable framework.*

*Some online drug stores offer vitamins to cure ED and concentrates on have demonstrated that Vitamin E might help men who likewise take Viagra - however conclusions are generally theoretical.*

*Vitamin supplements don't have symptoms, the length of measurements bearings are taken after painstakingly.*

## *Ginseng*

*Ginseng is a characteristic cure for ED which started in China. Concentrates on have demonstrated that it can have a mellow constructive outcome on weakness. On the other hand, ginseng might likewise bring down your glucose levels, which makes it exceptionally unsafe for diabetics. Try not to take it in the event that you think your ED might have been created by diabetes.*

## *"Home made" Viagra*

*Numerous items will claim to contain a home grown type of Viagra: these are regularly perilous and have been banned in the US and somewhere else in Europe. In the UK, search for the THR logo (customary natural enrollment) on the crate of the item. Unique, authorized Viagra is just accessible on solution. It is essential that you converse with a completely qualified specialist preceding taking it - this is to guarantee you get the most ideal treatment for your ED.Numerous self-broadcasted common cures for feebleness speak to "a genuine risk to general wellbeing and could be perilous", as the MHRA (Medicines and Healthcare items Regulatory Agency (UK)) states.Once more, the significance of counseling an expert specialist must be highlighted.*

*It is not worth finding an unsafe treatment on the web, when powerful and safe medicines can be lawfully recommended and got at a comparative cost - for instance from a controlled UK online specialist, for example, DrEd. Your ED might likewise hail up a genuine fundamental issue that additionally needs treatment: you have to counsel a GP for this.*

*The Food and Drug Administration has recorded various conceivably unsafe items to dodge that are frequently being sold under the classification of "regular cure for erectile dysfunction".A wellbeing treatment that is not delegated standard Western restorative practice is alluded to as "option" or "integral." Alternative medicines incorporate nutritious supplements, home grown cures, and needle therapy, for instance.*

*A few men might utilize elective medicines notwithstanding conventional medications for ED. In the event that you are considering an option type of treatment for ED, look for the counsel of a medicinal services supplier before beginning.*

## *Alternative Treatments for ED*

*Wholesome supplements: Nutritional supplements including the amino corrosive arginine, bioflavonoids, zinc, vitamin C, vitamin E, and flaxseed dinner have been utilized to enhance erectile capacity. Also, certain ED patients with low levels of the hormone dehydroepiandrosterone (DHEA) indicated change in erectile capacity in the wake of accepting supplemental dosages of DHEA. On the other hand, on the grounds that the long haul security of DHEA is not known, most specialists don't suggest its utilization.*

*Natural cures: Asian ginseng and Ginkgo biloba are accepted to enhance erectile capacity in a few men. Notwithstanding, counsel a specialist before taking any natural supplements to guarantee they are sheltered.*

## Acupuncture

*An old Chinese system for mending that includes staying fine, strong needles into particular focuses on the body, needle therapy invigorates the body's capacity to oppose or overcome diseases and conditions by remedying "lopsided characteristics." Acupuncture has helped a few men with ED.*

*On the off chance that you are having erection issues, counsel a specialist to decide the reason and find out about treatment choices.*

## Judgment skills Measures

*Remember that on the grounds that most option and integral medications are not controlled, it is hard to comprehend what you are getting. Here are a few tips to take after when considering utilizing home grown solutions for erectile dysfunction.*

*Converse with your specialist about any home grown items you are considering before attempting them.*

*On the off chance that you encounter symptoms, for example, queasiness, heaving, fast pulse, tension, a sleeping disorder, loose bowels, or skin rashes, quit taking the home grown item and tell your specialist.*

*Select brands deliberately. Just buy marks that rundown the herb's regular and logical name, the name and address of the maker, a bunch and part number, lapse date, dose rules, and potential symptoms.*

*Most importantly, if assuming control over-the-counter supplements, make sure your specialist is educated so you can maintain a strategic distance from antagonistic cooperations with physician recommended drugs you might be taking.*

# Chapter 14

## Natural herbs for premature ejaculation

*Sexual dreams can reach more prominent statures if a man can drag out his discharge. Managing discharge can likewise help in accomplishing more prominent fulfillment for your mate. Sad however it appears to be, numerous men experience the ill effects of untimely discharge which is a disappointment in drawing out the discharge and achieving full peak. Untimely discharge is more regular among more seasoned men. Be that as it may, it is likewise not an irregularity among the more youthful era of men.*

## Untimely Ejaculation

*Experiencing untimely discharge can prompt shame and absence of trust in men as they neglect to fulfill their accomplices and well as themselves. Because of this, numerous men don't look for treatment, not to mention discuss their issue. The uplifting news is this condition is exceptionally treatable at home without the assistance of a specialist. You can stay away from shame by taking the advantages of herbs that can improve things greatly in your sexual coexistence.*

*Before you attempt medicines that can prompt a large group of other symptoms and clutters, attempt these home grown cures that can renew your regenerative needs and keep you and your accomplice fulfilled also. An expression of exhortation however would be to sit tight for results to appear, as home grown and characteristic medicines take as much time as is needed to convey, yet convey they will, without a doubt!*

## Natural ways to cure premature ejaculation

### Onions

*Green onion seeds help as a love potion and thus can help in prolonging so as to control untimely discharge your sexual limits. Take a spoon of the seeds of green onions and add it to one glass of water. Blend well and drink this before each supper you have. This will enhance your stamina and energy to control your discharge.*

*The white assortment of onion too is an incredible love potion which can fortify the regenerative organs and anticipate untimely discharge. Onions can simply be bitten down your throat consistently to make the most of its advantages.*

### Ashwagandha

*An ayurvedic cure that is extremely prevalent in India, aswagandha can treat various sexual issues in men including the issue of untimely discharge.*

*The herb builds drive which is a critical component that aides in enhancing so as to control untimely discharge and drawing out sexual delight. Aswagandha gives physical stamina and treat erectile brokenness and barrenness.*

## *Ginger And Honey*

*Ginger aides in warming the body up and enhancing the blood dissemination. Devouring ginger enhances the blood stream to the penis also which is useful in holding the erection and avoiding untimely discharge.*

*Take a large portion of a teaspoon of ginger and the same measure of nectar and add this to a glass of warm drain. Drink this before you are set for overnight boardinghouse will unquestionably see the change.*

## *Lady finger*

*A powder got from lady finger is known not untimely discharge. Take around ten grams of the powder and add to a warm glass of milk. Blend two teaspoons of sweet sugar to this and drink this consistently night. Proceeding with this for a month in any event will give you astonishing change from your untimely discharge issue..*

## Raw Garlic

*Crude garlic also can help in treating untimely discharge and different issues in men. Biting 3-4 cloves of garlic can have a great deal of effect in your untimely discharge and help your stay solid also.*

*Garlic can be seared in immaculate dairy animals' ghee to expel the warmth from it and hold its love potion properties. Garlic will lessen erectile brokenness furthermore untimely discharge.*

## Carrots and eggs

*Slash two carrots and blend it with a half bubbled egg. Add one tablespoon of nectar to this. This can be taken each day for around three months. You will gradually feel a discernible distinction in your issue and will feel vastly improved following three months.*

*Once the untimely discharge is under control, you can lessen the admission of this cure.*

## Asparagus Root

*Untimely discharge can be regarded with asparagus root too. Take around 20 grams of asparagus root and bubble it alongside a glass of milk.*

*This intense milk can be devoured subsequent to depleting the root. Do this twice every day for controlling your untimely discharge and curing it at last.*

## Kegel Exercises

*Certain fortifying activities can help in enhancing your backbone and control your discharge. Kegel activities are activities that can reinforce the pelvic muscles that assistance in holding an erection furthermore in controlling untimely discharge. This is a simple practice that should be possible anyplace you are.*

*Stand straight and contract the muscles in your rump. It will be the same way you press your muscles to control pee. Hold it for 10 to 15 seconds and discharge it. This will fortify your pelvic muscles and enhance your capacity to control discharge. Do this 15-20 times each day for best results.*

## Characteristic Aphrodisiacs

*Characteristic aphrodisiacs can enhance your moxie and counteract untimely discharge. This would incorporate carrots, fennel seeds, celery, bananas, garlic, onion, ginger, shellfish, lettuce and so forth.*

## Carrots

*Counting these nourishments in your every day eating regimen will guarantee that you stay free from sexual issues, including untimely discharge.*

## Physical Methods

*Untimely discharge can be controlled by honing certain physical strategies at the season of intercourse. While you have sex, when you are going to get a climax, you can haul out your penis from the vagina and sit tight for around 30 seconds. You might re enter after this, which will offer you some assistance with retaining your discharge for more time furthermore offer you some assistance with getting more control over your erection.*

## Castor Oil

*Untimely discharge in more established men can be the aftereffect of issues identified with the prostate. To control prostate issues and to keep its event, castor oil can be utilized for kneading into the prostate organ.*

www.ingramcontent.com/pod-product-compliance
Ingram Content Group UK Ltd.
Pitfield, Milton Keynes, MK11 3LW, UK
UKHW041942190726
13854UKWH00004B/1735